Learn to Speak and Write ARABIC

Published by
Lotus Press Publishers & Distributors

Learn to Speak and Write ARABIC

Md. Ziaullah
Jawaharlal Nehru University
New Delhi

Lotus Press
4735/22, Prakash Deep Building
Ansari Road, Darya Ganj,
New Delhi - 110002

Lotus Press : Publishers & Distributors
Unit No. 220, 2nd Floor, 4735/22, Prakash Deep Building,
Ansari Road, Darya Ganj, New Delhi- 110002
Ph.: 32903912, 23280047, 98188-38000
• E-mail : lotuspress1984@gmail.com
www.lotuspress.co.in

Learn to Speak and Write Arabic

ISBN: 978-81-8382-311-1

Printed & Published by : **Lotus Press Publisher & Distributors,** New Delhi-02

About the Book

In the modern era of our time where the globalization has rendered the boarders between the countries meaningless, a floating world population has emerged which keeps shifting from one place to another and a mass movement is always going on. This unique juncture in the history of human civilization has ushered in immense changes in outlook and has brought many cultures together at a stage where they are forced to co-exist with each other and negotiate with tough situations to create equilibrium for the benefit of all but still the world remains a place where the contestation is a reality of everyday life. This contestation has pushed the boundaries of debate and necessitated that the whole issue is looked into from different angles. Besides this aspect of the modern globalised world, economic and cultural aspects have their own set of issues which keep the prominent leaders in many fields engaged in providing solutions to these intriguing problems. In this whole debate of contestation and power tussle, the Arab world is major player not only because of its immense natural wealth and strategic location but also because it has been and continues to be the land of great civilizations and three great religions of the world: Islam, Judaism and Christianity. At this point the language plays central role in understanding the culture, interacting with the people at large and pursuing economic and commercial interests.

Arabic Language and Culture are very important also due to the Arab Countries' strategic location and its oil and natural wealth which play pivotal role in the economy and politics of a globalised world order. Knowing Arabic is always useful for businessmen, professionals, scholars doing research on the region and many others. Arabic is spoken by the people of more than twenty countries of the World. What underscores its importance further is the fact that it is one of the official languages of the United Nations. Keeping these realities in mind this book is aimed at providing help to the beginners to learn Arabic through some effective steps and easy to understand techniques. A practical and step by step approach has been adopted in this book to simplify the most intriguing part of the Arabic language i.e. grammar, keeping in view the target groups of businessmen, professionals and general readers interested in the region of the Middle East.

There are many books on Arabic grammar and composition in the market and many great scholars of this language have given their best to it and "there is nothing new in a book of grammar" as a great teacher and author of Arabic from India Professor Rafi'el-Imad Faynan rightly says "except its presentation and its ability to effectively and smoothly communicate ideas to the mind of a beginner". Still, what makes this book different from all the existing writing on the topic is it's easy to grasp method of explaining the complex issues of Arabic grammar where two plus two is equal to four method of mathematical analysis has been adopted which makes language learning an interesting experience. The author found this method extremely useful during his teaching assignment at Bharti Vidya Bhavan in New Delhi where he had to teach some brilliant students from non-Arabic background and they showed visible results in a very short period of time. This book is also unique in the sense that it provides lots of examples using words of daily usage. Even the traditional order in Arabic grammar has been shunned as it appears from the table of the content. The book has been divided into three main parts:

The first part deals with Arabic grammar and its application through model sentences and structural analysis of the sentence formation.

The second part contains conversations on different topics along with a long list of vocabularies.

The third part of it is exclusively devoted to word power building where many important words have been given alongside the terminologies used in the media.

The book gives priority to the needs of the beginners interested in learning Arabic for different purposes but it also takes care of the need of those who are working in the newly emerged sector of medical tourism and also of those who find reading Arabic newspapers and magazines difficult in a limited manner. I must acknowledge at this stage that during my teaching assignment the book of Arabic grammar written by Professor Rafi'el-Imad Faynan was very useful and any slight influence on the writing of this book might be because of that enriching experience. However, for conjugations in this book the pattern of Antuwan Al-Dahdah's book has been followed with slight modifications. Another author and teacher who had a genuine impact is our student-friendly Professor (now retired) Syed Ahsanur Rahman at JNU. Again his book, "Teach yourself Arabic" was my first experience of learning Arabic through modern method when I moved to University system of education. Before that Nadwatul Ulama, the world famous institute of Arabic literature and Islamic studies, played major role in producing many greats in the field of Arabic literature and culture studies. I feel humbled to belong to these two institutes of excellence in their own right.

The author owes thanks to many people who played their role in making this book a reality. My first thank goes to my simple living parents and my beloved wife who were great sources of support and encouragement during the writing of this book. My friend Nabiel Ansari deserves special thanks for introducing me to the very candid and supportive owner of Lotus Publications, Mr. A. J. Sehgal, who was always ready to support. Without his constant encouragement this book would not have seen the light of the day. My mentor for the research work at JNU Dr. Rizwanur Rahman is always a big source of assistance and valuable suggestions. Last but not the least, my thank also goes to two of my friends, Dr. Naseem Ahmad and Dr. Akhtar Alam , with whom I discussed some of the chapters of the book. However, for any sort of mistake in the book solely the author takes the moral responsibility.

Md. Ziaullah

Table of content

PART (I) : Arabic Grammar and Application

Chapter 1 : Alphabets and words formations
Chapter 2 : Gender
Chapter 3 : Definite and indefinite nouns
Chapter 4 : Vowel marks
Chapter 5 : Singular, dual and plural
Chapter 6 : Demonstrative pronouns
Chapter 7 : Subject and predicate
Chapter 8 : Noun qualified and adjective
Chapter 9 : Possessed and possessor
Chapter 10 : Prepositions
Chapter 11 : Particles of interrogation
Chapter 12 : Particles of emphasis
Chapter 13 : Conjugations of weak verbs
Chapter 14 : Kinds of sentences
Chapter 15 : Past tense and its conjugations
Chapter 16 : Present / Future tense and its conjugations
Chapter 17 : Negative of past tense
Chapter 18 : Negative of present/ future tense
Chapter 19 : Subject and object
Chapter 20 : Imperative verb
Chapter 21 : Negative imperative verb
Chapter 22 : Passive voice
Chapter 23 : Verbal noun

Chapter 24 : Some important uses:
Has/ have + third form of the verb
Has to / have to
Has / have
Chapter 25 : Relative pronouns
Chapter 26 : List of conjugations
Chapter 27 : Exceptions in Arabic grammar
Chapter 28 : Number and Al-ma-du-du

PART (II) : Conversation

(1) Useful greetings and courtesies
(2) At home with family and friend
(3) Receiving the friend at the station
(4) Booking room in a hotel
(5) Dinner in a restaurant
(6) In the market
(7) In the cinema
(8) At the dispensary
(9) At the railway station
(10) At the airport
(11) Opening a bank account

PART (III) : Extra word power

This part include words as per the below detail

- Fruits
- Vegetables
- Spices
- Animals
- Birds
- Colors
- Body parts

- Human relations
- Seasons and directions
- Profession
- Days and months
- Things related to time and days
- Words and terms used in the media

PART ONE
ARABIC GRAMMAR AND APPLICATION

Chapter 1
Alphabets of Arabic

As we know that the basics of any language start with alphabets of that particular language. It is because these alphabets are the building blocks of any language. Likewise, Arabic also has its alphabets as below:

Alif	A	ا
Baa	B	ب
Taa	T	ت
Tha	Th	ث
Jeem	J	ج
Haa	H	ح
Kha	Kh	خ
Daal	D	د
Dhal	Dh	ذ
Raa	R	ر
Zaa	Z	ز
Seen	S	س
Sheen	Sh	ش
Saad	S	ص
Dhaad	D.	ض
Taa'	T	ط
Dhaa	Z	ظ
Ay'n	A'	ع
Ghay'n	Gh	غ
Faa	F	ف

Qaaf	Q	ق
Kaaf	K	ك
Laam	L	ل
Meem	M	م
Nun	N	ن
Waw	W	و
Haa	H	ه
Ya	Y	ى

How to form a word (a)

Once you know the alphabets and their pronunciation, the next stage in the learning process comes when you have to know how to connect the letters with each other to form a WORD. So, how to form a Word? Let us learn it in an easy way.

Short vowels

But before you embark on this and take up the task of forming words, you must know about the tools which will assist you in this regard. The tools are as below. Look at them carefully and recognize them well as these will come handy every time you want to form a word and beyond.

These are called short vowels. Without vowels you cannot form or pronounce a word in Arabic. Short vowels are "Damma" (بُ)"Fatha" , (بَ) "Kasra" (بِ)and "Sukun" (بْ).

So we will say (lu) لُ, (du) دُ, and (bu) بُ with "Damma"
(di) دِ, (qi) قِ, and حِ (hi) with "Kasra" and
سَ (sa) لَ (la) and مَ (ma) with "Fatha"

Look at the below column. This will give you better idea about the short vowels and how they are pronounced as few more examples are added to this:

Kasra	Fatha	Damma
(Ti) طِ, (Ni) نِ, (Ghi) غِ	(Fa) فَ, (La) لَ, (Ta) تَ	(Thu) ثُ, (Khu) خُ, (Du) دُ

(Khi) خِ, (Li) لِ, (Qi) قِ	(Dha) ضَ, (Ra) رَ, (Ba) بَ	(Mu) مُ, (Ru) رُ, (Dhu) ظُ
(Fi) فِ, (Mi) مِ, (Di) دِ	(Sa) سَ, (Ka) كَ, (Za) زَ	(Ku) كُ, (Tu) تُ, (Lu) لُ
(Ki) كِ, (Ti) تِ, (Si) سِ	(Sha) شَ, (Ta) طَ, (Na) نَ	(Su) سُ, (Hu) حُ, (Nu) نُ
(Shi) شِ, (Bi) بِ, (Ji) جِ	(Ma) مَ, (Qa) قَ, (Tha) ثَ	(Zu) زُ, (Bu) بُ, (Ju) جُ

Long Vowels

Besides the short vowels, there is another group of vowels which are called "Long Vowels". These are as below:

(Waw) (و) واو
(Alif) اَلف (ا)
(Ya') (ي) ياء

Short vowel "Damma" ()is used with long vowel واو (Waw) and pronounced as below:

(Boo) بُو
(Shoo) شُو
(Loo) لُو

Short vowel "Fatha" ()is used along with the long vowel ا لف (Alif) and pronounced as under:

(Baa) بَا
(Faa) فَا
(Maa) مَا

As far as short vowel "Kasra" is concerned, it is used along with ياء (Ya') and pronounced as below:

(Fii) فِي
(Jii) جِي
(Kii) كِي

Practice the vowels by trying to recognize them from the below examples.

فُ بَ طِ نُ شَ صُ تِ حَ دِ عُ خَ ء ى كِ سُ رَ وُ ةِ جَ ثِ هُ ذِل ضَ غُ مَ ظِ قُ زَ اِ
فَا, مَا, شِي, ثُو, كِي, بَا, لاَ, دِي, سَا, بُو,فِي,لُو, كُو, جَا, نِي, عَا, حُو, دِي, شُو,مُو

Things to remember

1. English is written from left to right, however, Arabic is written from right to left.
2. There are two kinds of vowels i.e. (a) short vowels which are "Damma" , (اُ) "Fatha" (اَ)and "Kasra", (اِ).
3. Long vowels which are واو (Waw) , الف (Alif) and يا ء (Ya')

How to Form Word (b)

In the previous pages you read about the first stage in forming a word. Here are few more tools without which one cannot be able to form a word. These are called "Orthographic signs" and are considered to be vital in this regard. These are as under:

(a) Madda Example: آل (Aal) , آم (Aam)

(b) Sukun (بْ)" " " بَلْ : (Bal) , جَلْ (Jal)

(c) Shadda) (لّ " " " : ظَلَّ (Zal-la) , (قَلَّ)(Qal-la)

(d) Tanween (اً,اٍ,اٌ)" " " : وَلَدٌ (Wa-la-dun) , رَجُلاً (Ra-ju-lan) and بَيْتٍ (Bay-tin) .

MADDA

Let us deal with every "Orthographic sign" one by one so it may give a better idea how it works."Madda" replaces double الف (Ali) with a single one and orthographic sign "Madda" is put on the head of الف, so ا+ا becomes آ. Look at the examples below:

ا+ا+ل=آلْ (Aal)

ا+ا+م= آمْ (Aam)

ا+ا+ب= آبْ (Aab)

SHADDA

The Orthographic sign "Shadda" means that if a letter carries this sign then such letter will be pronounced twice however it will be written just once. Example:

مَ+دْ+دَ = مَدَّ (Mad-da)

قَ+لْ+لَ = قَلَّ (Qal-la)

شَ+طْ+طَ = شَطَّ (Shat-ta)

You can see that the letters with Orthographic Sign "Shadda" in the above examples have been pronounced twice.

SUKUN

Orthographic sign "SUKUN" denotes the state of being vowel-less and any letter carrying this sign will always be pronounced along with a letter coming before it. The sybol of "SUKUN" is ْ. Have a look at the below examples to know more about it:

قَبْلُ = قَ+بْ+لُ

حَبْلُ =حَ+بْ+لُ

فَوْقُ = فَ+وْ+قُ

قَصْرُ = قَ+صْ+رُ

In the examples given above, letters "ب", "و" and "ص" are vowel-less and have been pronounced jointly with the letters preceding these letters.

TAN-WEEN

Tanween is called "Nunation" and gives the sound of "N" to the last letter of the word and is written in three different ways. These are as below:

(1) Tanween with "Damma" (اٌ) gives the sound of "un" like:
Raju-lun (رَجُلٌ) , Kutu-bun (كُتُبٌ) , Bin-tun (بِنْتٌ) ,

(2) Tanween with "Fatha" (اً)gives the sound of "an" as in:
Raju-lan (رَجُلاً) , Kutu-ban (كُتُباً) , Bin-tan (بِنْتاً) ,

Tanween with "Kasra" (اٍ)gives the sound of "in" like in:
Raju-lin (رَجُلٍ) , Kutu-bin (كُتُبٍ) , Bin-tin (بِنْتٍ)

Things to remember

Please note that "Tanween with Fatha" is always written along with "ا" (Alif) so it can carry "Nunation" with ease. This alif always comes in the end. (See the examples)

Chapter 2
Gender

In the previous chapter you read about the formation of words. In this chapter you are going to read about "Gender". Observe the below given examples to understand it well.

Masculine	Feminine
طَالِبٌ (Tali-bun)	طَالِبَةٌ (Tali-ba-tun)
صَغِيَرٌ (Sa-ghee-run)	صَغِيْرَةٌ (Sa-ghee-ra-tun)
جَمِيْلٌ (Ja-mi-lun)	جَمِيْلَةٌ (Ja-mi-la-tun)

By looking at the above examples you can understand and differentiate between a masculine as well as a feminine noun and adjective. It is very important to know how to recognise a masculine from a feminine one.

Any Arabic word ending with round "ة" (Ta) is called "Feminine" or Al-mu-an-nas (المُؤَنَثْ) in Arabic like:

kabi-ra-tun (كَبِيْرَةٌ) Big

Sa-ghee-ra-tun (صَغِيْرَةٌ) Small

Ta-wee-la-tun (طَوِيْلَةٌ) Tall

Likewise, if you remove the round "ة" (Ta) from the end of the word it becomes "Masculine" or Al-mu-zak-kar (المُذَكّر) , hence:

Kabi-ra-tun (كَبِيْرَةٌ) becomes Kabi-run (كَبِيْرٌ) and Sa-ghee-ra-tun (صَغِيْرَةٌ) becomes Sa-ghee-ru (صَغِيْرٌ)

Let us practice some examples to have a proper understanding about "Gender". The below column will help you understand المُذَكّرْ as well as المُؤَنَثْ.

Masculine (الْمُذكّر)	**Feminine (الْمُؤنّث)**
طِفْلٌ (Tif-lun) a child سَائِقٌ (Sai-qun) a male driver خَادِمٌ (Kha-di-mun) a male servant سَمِيْنٌ (Sa-mi-nun) a fat man هَذِيْلٌ (Ha-zi-lun) a thin man حَزِيْنٌ (Hazi-nun) a sad man جَمِيْلٌ (Jami-lun) a smart man	طِفْلة (Tif-la-tun) a girl child سَائِقَة (Sai-qa-tun) a female driver خَادِمَة (Kha-di-ma-tun) a maid servant سَمِيْنَة (Sa-mi-na-tun) a fat woman هَذِيْلَة (Ha-zi-la-tun) a thin woman حَزِيْنَة (Hazi-na-tun) a sad woman جَمِيْلَة (Jami-la-tun) a beautiful woman.

Exercise

Find out masculine and feminine words from the below given examples

1. صَادِقٌ (an honest person)
2. كَاذِبٌ (a liar)
3. طوِيْلَة (tall)
4. مَرِيْضٌ (a patient)
5. صَادِقَة (an honest person)
6. صَالِحَة (a pious person)
7. طوِيْلٌ (tall)
8. ثَمِيْنَة (fat)
9. مَاهِرٌ (an expert)

Chapter 3
Definite and indefinite nouns

Go through the below mentioned examples to understand "Article" in Arabic and its application in it:

Definite Noun (اَلْمَعْرِفَة)	Indefinite Noun (اَلنَّكِرَةُ)
اَلوَلَدُ (Al-wa-la-du) The boy	وَلَدٌ (Wa-la-dun) A boy
اَلبِنْتُ (Al-bin-tu) The girl	بِنْتٌ (Bin-tun) A girl
اَلبَيْتُ (Al-ba'y-tu) The house	بَيْتٌ (Ba'y-tun) A house

The examples you read in the above box shows that a "Definite" noun starts with "Article" (اَلْ) and the last letter does not carry "Nunation". On the contrary, an indefinite noun starts without (اَلْ) and ends with "Nunation".

It also indicates that the English Article "The" has its equivalent in Arabic as "اَل" and the same way Articles "a" and "an" have their equivalent in Arabic as "Nunation" or Tanween.

So, if you want to turn an indefinite noun into a definite one as per the Arabic grammar you have to prefix "اَل" to that particular noun. Therefore:

رَجُلٌ (a man) becomes اَلرَّجُلُ (the man)

كِتَابٌ (a book) " " " " اَلكِتَابُ (the book)

قلمٌ (a pen) becomes اَلقلمُ (the pen)

قمِيْصٌ (a shirt) " " " اَلقمِيْصُ (the shirt)

مَنْزِلٌ (a house) " " اَلمَنْزِلُ (the house)

رَئِيسٌ (a chief) "" اَلرَّئِيسُ (the chief)

Sun and Moon Letters

You have already recognized the below mentioned letters when you went through the chapter on alphabets. But now you should keep these letters in your mind for a different reason altogether.

ت,ث,د, ذ, ر, ز, س, ش, ص, ض, ط, ظ, ن

If an indefinite Arabic noun starts with any of the above mentioned letters and you want to turn that noun into a definite one by prefixing (al) "الْ" to it, in that case the letter "ل" (lam) of "الْ" (al) will not be pronounced, instead the letter immediately following "ل" (lam) will be pronounced twice because of carrying "Shad-da" (دّ). See the example as under:

Meaning	Pronunciation	Definite	Indefinite	Sun letters
Repentant	At-ta-i-bu	التَّائِبُ	تَائِبٌ	ت
Wealth	As-sar-va-tu	الثَّرْوَةُ	ثَرْوَةٌ	ث
State	Ad-dau-la-tu	الدَّوْلَةُ	دَوْلَةٌ	د
Defense	Adh-dhaud-du	الذَّوْدُ	ذَوْدٌ	ذ
Subsistence	Ar-riz-qu	الرِّزْقُ	رِزْقٌ	ر
Oil	Az-zay-tu	الزَّيْتُ	زَيْتٌ	ز
Market	As-suu-qu	السُّوْقُ	سُوْقٌ	س
Thank	Ash-shuk-ru	الشُّكْرُ	شُكْرٌ	ش
Hunting	As-say-du	الصَّيْدُ	صَيْدٌ	ص
Bandage	Az-zam-du	الضَّمْدُ	ضَمْدٌ	ض
Bird	At-tay-ru	الطَّيْرُ	طَيْرٌ	ط
Gazelle	Az-zab-yu	الظَّبْيُ	ظَبْيٌ	ظ
Light	An-noo-ru	النُّوْرُ	نُوْرٌ	ن

Arabic word صَخْرٌ (Sakh-run) will be pronounced as الصَّخْرُ and ثَرْوَةٌ will be pronounced as الثَّرْوَةُ. You can practice all other words starting with the above alphabets keeping these examples in mind. These letters are called sun letters and rest of the alphabets are called moon letters because they do not influence the pronuniciation of the words like sun letters.

Things to remember

*Definite noun does not carry "Nunation" or Tanween.

*Indefinite noun does not carry Article "الْ"

*Definite noun is called "الْمَعْرِفَة" in Arabic

*Indefinite noun is called "النَّكِرَةٌ" in Arabic

Exercise

Try to find out definite and indefinite nouns from the words given as below:

1. اَلْكَلْبُ (Al-kal-bu) The dog
2. قِطَّةٌ (Qit-ta-tun) A cat
3. الأَسَدُ (Al-asa-du) The lion
4. نَجْمٌ (Naj-mun) A star
5. مُمَثِّلَةٌ (Mu-math-thi-la-tun) An actress
6. الْمُدِيْرُ (L-mu-di-ru) The Director

Chapter 4
The Three cases in Arabic- vowel marks

Nominative Case	Accusative Case	Genitive Case
رَجُلٌ (Ra-ju-lun)	رَجُلاً (Ra-ju-lan)	رَجُلٍ (Ra-ju-lin)
اَلرَّجُلُ (Ar-ra-ju-lu)	اَلرَّجُلَ (Ar-ra-ju-la)	اَلرَّجُلِ (Al-ra-ju-li)
وَكِيْلٌ, (Wa-ki-lun)	وَكِيْلاً, (Wa-ki-lan)	وَكِيْلٍ, (Wa-ki-lin)
الوَكِيلُ (Al-wa-kilu)	الوَكِيلَ (Al-wa-ki-la)	الوَكِيلِ (Al-wa-ki-li)

It is very essential for a student of Arabic language to know about the three cases of Arabic as they are very fundamental because the whole grammar revolves around these cases. These cases are:

(1) Nominative case
(2) Accusative case and
(3) Genitive case

In **Nominative case**, "Dam-ma" or "Dam-ma with Nunation" is applied on the last letter of the word.

Example:

- "Dam-ma" applies on the definite noun of Arabic as in (الوَرَقُ) (Al-wa-ra-qu) and (اَلكِتَابُ) (al-kita-bu) .
- "Dam-ma with Nunation" applies on an indefinite noun like (حَجَرٌ) (Ha-ja-run) and (قَلَمٌ) (Qala-mun) .

In **Accusative case**, "Fat-ha" or "Fat-ha with Nunation" is applied on the last letter of the word.

- "Fat-ha" is applied on the last letter of a definite noun as in (اَلبَابَ) (Al-ba-ba) and (القَمَرَ) (Al-qa-ma-ra) .
- "Fat-ha with Nunation" is applied on an indefinite noun as in (رَجُلاً) (Ra-ju-lan) and (دَرْساً) (Dar-san) .

In **Genitive case**, "Kas-ra" or "Kas-ra with Nunation" is applied on the last letter of the word. Example:

- "Kas-ra" is applied on the last letter of a definite noun as in (اَلبَيْتِ) (Al-bay'ti) and (الفَصْلِ) .
- "Kas-ra with Nunation" is applied on an indefinite noun as in (رَئِيْسٍ) (Raii-sin) and (صَدِيْقٍ) .

This variation in the last letter of a word takes place as per the position of that word in a sentence. This variation is called either "اَلإِعْرَاب" or "اَلتَّشْكِيْل" in Arabic grammar. The below column will help you understand why this variation takes place. However, things will be clearer only in the chapters to be followed. Observe the examples given below carefully:

Nominative case	Accusative Case	Genitive Case
أكَلَ الوَلَدُ	أكَلتُ الطَعَامَ	فِيْ السُّوْقِ
البِنْتُ جَمِيْلَة	كَانَتِ البِنْتُ جَمِيْلَة	عَلى الكُرْسِيٍّ

Chapter 5
Singular, Dual and Plural

In this chapter you will learn about "Singular", "Dual" and "Plural". Unlike English, Arabic grammar has certain specific rules for "Dual" also besides "Singular" and "Plural". First look at the below examples to familiarize yourself with the forms of all three:

Singular	Dual	Plural
اَلْوَلَدُ /وَلَدٌ	اَلْوَلَدَانِ/ وَلَدَانِ	اَلأَوْلَادُ/ أَوْلَادٌ
اَلرَّجُلُ / رَجُلٌ	اَلرَّجُلَانِ / رَجُلَانِ	اَلرِّجَالُ / رِجَالٌ
اَلْبِنْتُ / بِنْتٌ	اَلْبِنْتَانِ / بِنْتَانِ	اَلْبَنَاتُ / بَنَاتٌ
اَلصَّادِقُ / صَادِقٌ	اَلصَّادِقَانِ/ صَادِقَانِ	اَلصَّادِقُوْنَ/ صَادِقُوْنَ
اَلنَّاجِحَةُ / نَاجِحَةٌ	اَلنَّاجِحَتَانِ/ نَاجِحَتَانِ	اَلنَّاجِحَاتُ/ نَاجِحَاتٌ

By observing the above mentioned examples you can realize that Plural in Arabic has no set pattern and it keeps changing as per the whims and fancies. However, it is not so. You will know about the numerous patterns of Plural in Arabic. But let us deal with "Dual" first as it has a set pattern in Arabic.

By observing the above examples of "Dual" once again you can realize that "Dual" has been made on a fixed pattern. The pattern is as below:

The Singular noun is suffixed by ن+ا and it turns into Dual noun. The ن of "Dual" always carries vowel mark "Kasra" and the letter before (ا) اَلِفْ always carries vowel mark "Fatha". See some more examples in the below column to understand how "Dual" is made by suffixing: ن+ا

Singular	Dual
صَغِيْرٌ (A small person)	صَغِيْر + ان = صَغِيْرَانِ (Two small persons)
طِفْلَة (A girl child)	طِفْلَة + ان = طِفْلَتَانِ (Two girl children)
مُسْلِمٌ (A Muslim Man)	مُسْلِمَ + ان =مُسْلِمَانِ (Two Muslim Men)
خُبْزٌ (One bread)	خُبْزَ + ان = خُبْزَانِ (Two breads)

You must also remember that "Dual" is made by suffixing ان to the singular ONLY IN NOMINATIVE case. As far as ACCUSATIVE and GENITIVE cases are concerned, then the (ا) اَلِفْ of Dual is changed with ي and vowel mark "SUKUN" is given to this يْ, hence:

صَغِيْرَان becomes صَغِيْرَيْن

مُسْلِمَان " " " " مُسْلِمَيْن

وَلَدَان " " " " وَلَدَيْن and رَجُلَان becomes رَجُلَيْن .

Things to remember:

*Singular is called (Al-muf-ra-du) المُفْرَدُ in Arabic

*Dual is called (Al-mu-than-na) المُثَنّي and

*Plural is called (Al-jam-uu) الجَمْعُ

*"Damma" or "Damma with Nunation" on the last letter of Singular noun is replaced with "Fatha" while turning the Singular into dual noun.

*ن of Dual always carries vowel mark "Kasra".

How to make PLURAL

There are many ways of making Plural from a Singular noun. It is made from "Singular" by suffixing (وْنَ)to it in "Nominative Case" as in:

Singular (اَلْمُفْرَدْ)	Plural (اَلْجَمْعْ)
سَائِقٌ (Sai-qun)	(سَائِقٌ+وْنَ) سَائِقُوْنَ =
عَامِلٌ (Aa-mi-lun)	(عَامِلُ+وْنَ) = عَامِلُوْنَ

As you can see in the above examples that the singular nouns (عَامِلٌ) and (سَائِقٌ) have been turned into Plural by suffixing (وْنَ) to it. The letter وَاوْ carries verbal mark "SUKUN" whereas the ن carries vowel mark "Fat-ha" on it. The "Damma with Nunation" on the last letter of a Singular noun is replaced with "Damma" while making Plural.

In "Accusative" and "Genitive" cases the "Plural" is made from a "Singular Noun" as per below pattern by suffixing (يْنَ) يْ+نَ to it as in:

Singular (اَلْمُفْرَدُ)	Plural (اَلْجَمْعُ)
سَائِقٌ (Sai-qun) عَامِلٌ (Aa-mi-lun)	(سَائِق+يْنَ) = سَائِقِيْنَ (عَامِل+يْنَ) = عامِلِيْنَ

You can see that in these two cases Plural has been made by adding (يْنَ)to the last letter of the Singular noun. In this case the letter before "ي" always carries "Kasra" and the letter "ن" always carries "Fat-ha".

Some more patterns of PLURAL

There are some more patterns of "Plural" about which you will learn in the following column. These patterns are fixed one. Any Singular noun coming on that particular pattern will be turned into Plural as per the pattern of Plural given below:

Pattern-1

Pattern of Singular	Pattern of Plural is: (فُعَّالٌ)
حَاكِمٌ (A Ruler) كَاتِبٌ (A Writer) رَاكِبٌ (A Rider)	حُكَّامٌ كُتَّابٌ رُكَّابٌ

Pattern-2

Pattern of Singular	Pattern of Plural is: (فُعَلاءُ)
زَعِيْمٌ (A Leader) شَرِيْفٌ (A Noble man) كَرِيْمٌ (A Kind Person)	زُعَمَاءُ شُرَفَاءُ كُرَمَاءُ

Pattern-3

Pattern of Singular	Pattern of Plural is: (فُعُوْلٌ)
لَيْثٌ (A Lion) مَيْلٌ (Inclination) بَيْتٌ (A House)	لُيُوْثٌ مُيُوْلٌ بُيُوْتٌ

Pattern-4

Pattern of Singular	Pattern of Plural is: (مَفَاعِلُ)
مَكْتَبٌ (An Office)	مَكَاتِبُ
مَعْبَدٌ (A Temple)	مَعَابِدُ
مَصْنَعٌ (A Factory)	مَصَانِعُ

Pattern-5

Pattern of Singular	Pattern of Plural is: (أَفْعَالٌ)
شَجَرٌ (A Tree)	أَشْجَارٌ
قَلَمٌ (A Pen)	أَقْلَامٌ
زَهَرٌ (A Flower)	اَزْهَارٌ

Besides those above given patterns there are some other patterns like:
فِعَالٌ, فَعَالٌ, فَعْلَي and others about which you will learn on the journey towards perfection in Arabic language. However, a list of Singular as well as Plural nouns is being given below for your benefit. Go through all these and memorize them so you can use them in your daily conversation confidently.

Singular Noun	Plural Noun
ضَيْفٌ (Dhai-fun)	ضُيُوْفٌ (Dhu-yu-fu) Guests
سُوْقٌ (Su-qun)	أَسْوَاقٌ (As-wa-qun) Markets
طِفْلٌ (Tif-lun)	أَطْفَالٌ (At-fa-lun) Children
دَرْسٌ (Dar-sun)	دُرُوْسٌ (Du-ru-sun) Lessons
سَيَّارَةٌ (Say-ya-ra-tun)	سَيَّارَاتٌ (Say-ya-ra-tun) Cars
مَحَطَّةٌ (Ma-hat-ta-tun)	مَحَطَّاتٌ (Ma-hat-ta-tun) Stations
صَنْدُوْقٌ (Sun-du-qun)	صَنَادِيْقُ (Sa-na-di-qu) Boxes
كَلْبٌ (Kal-bun)	كِلَابٌ (Ki-la-bun) Dogs

قِطَّةٌ (Qit-ta-tun)	قِطَطٌ (Qit-ta-tun) Cats
شَهْرٌ (Shah-run)	شُهُوْرٌ (Shu-hoo-run) Months
سَنَةٌ (Sana-tun)	سِنِيْنَ/سِنُوْنَ (Sinoo-na) Years
أُسْبُوْعٌ (Us-bu-un)	أَسَابِيْعُ (Asa-bi-a) Weeks
وَكِيْلٌ (Wakee-lun)	وُكَلَاءُ (Wo-ka-la-u) Agents
طَبِيْبٌ (Tabi-bun)	أَطِبَّاءُ (Atib-ba-u) Doctors
مُهَنْدِسٌ (Muhan-di-sun)	مُهَنْدِسُوْنَ (Mu-han-di-suna) Engineers
عَالِمٌ (Ali-mun)	عُلَمَاءُ (Ula-ma-u) LearnedPersons/ Scientists
زَمِيْلٌ (Zami-lun)	زُمَلَاءُ (Zu-ma-la-u) Colleagues
مَدِيْنَةٌ (Madi-na-tun)	مُدُنٌ (Mu-du-nun) Cities
عَاصِمَةٌ (Asi-ma-tun)	عَوَاصِمُ (Awa-si-mu) Capitals
مَدْرَسَةٌ (Mad-ra-sa-tun)	مَدَارِسُ (Ma-da-ri-su) Schools
جَامِعَةٌ (Jami-a-tun)	جَامِعَاتٌ (Jami-aa-tun) Universities
كُلِّيَةٌ (Kul-li-ya-tun)	كُلِّيَاتٌ (Kul-li-ya-tun) Colleges

Exercise-1

Make dual from the following Singular nouns:

1. مَنْزِلٌ (A House)
2. مَدِيْنَةٌ (A City)
3. شُبَّاكٌ (A Window)
4. بَابٌ (A Door)
5. قُفْلٌ (A Lock)
6. مِفْتَاحٌ (A Key)

Exercise-2

Make Plural from the below given Singular Nouns:

1. رَازِقٌ (One who bestows)
2. مَاكِرٌ (A Cunning Person)
3. دَاخِلٌ (An Entrant)
4. بَاطِلٌ (Untrue)

Chapter 6
The Demonstrative Pronouns

Look at the below pronouns. These are very important and useful for expressions.

Demonstrative pronouns for near:

Masculine	Feminine	Masculine/Feminine
هٰذَا (Ha-za) (S) This هٰذَان (Ha-za-ni) (D) These Two	هٰذِہٖ (Ha-zi-hi) (S) This هَاتَان (Ha-ta-ni) (D) These Two	هٰؤلاءِ (Ha-uu-la-i) (P) These Persons

As you can see in the above column, the "Demonstrative Pronoun" for Plural is the same for both "Masculine" as well as "Feminine.

HOW TO USE:

To know how to use the above given "Demonstrative Pronouns" you should go through the following examples (1) (a) .

Example (1) (a) :

Masculine Singular	Masculine Dual	Masculine Plural
هَذَا+البَيْتُ = هَذَاالبَيْتُ هَذَا+الرَّجُلُ = هَذَالرَّجُلُ هَذَا+المُدِيْرُ = هَذَالمُدِيْرُ	هَذَان+ البَيْتَا ن = هَذَان البَيْتَان هَذَان+الرَّجُلَان =هَذَان الرَّجُلَان هَذَان+المُدِيْرَان=هَذَان المُدِيْرَان	هٰؤُلَاءِ+الرِّجَالُ=هٰؤُلَاءِالرِّجَالُ هٰؤُلَاءِ+البَنَاتُ =هٰؤُلَاءِالبَنَاتُ

So, the meaning of (هَذَاالرَّجُلُ) will be "This Man". Likewise, the meaning of (هَذَاالبَيْتُ) will be "This House" and the meaning of (هَذَاالمُدِيْرُ) will be "This Director" in Singular Case.

In Dual Case, the meaning of (هَذَان الرَّجُلَان) will be "These Two Men" and the meaning of (هٰؤُلَاءِالرِّجَالُ) will be "These Men" in Plural Case.

Example (1) (b) :

Feminine Singular	Feminine Dual	Feminine Plural
هَذِهِ+المُدَرِّسَةُ = هَذِهِ المُدَرِّسَةُ	هَاتَانِ+المُدَرِّسَتَانِ= هَاتَانِ المُدَرِّسَتَانِ	هَؤُلَاءِ+المُدَرِّسَا تُ = هَؤُلَاءِالمُدَرِّسَاتُ

Here also, the meaning of (هَذِهِ المُدَرِّسَةُ) will be "This lady teacher" in Singular case whereas the Dual case (هَاتَانِ المُدَرِّسَتَانِ) will mean as "These Two lady teachers" and the Plural Case (هَؤُلَاءِالمُدَرِّسَاتُ) will mean as "These lady teachers".

Demonstrative pronoun for distant:

Masculine	Feminine	Masculine/Feminine
ذَالِكَ (Za-li-ka) (S) That ذَانِكَ (Za-ni-ka) (D) Those Two	تِلْكَ (Til-ka) (S) That تَانِكَ (Ta-ni-ka) (D) Those Two	أُولَئِكَ (Uu-la-i-ka) (P) Those People

Now look at another set of examples below which will give you more clarity about the "Demonstrative Pronouns". For convenience this is being called example (2) (a) .

Example (2) (a) :

Masculine Singular	Masculine Dual	Masculine Plural
ذَالِكَ+ الوَلَدُ=ذَالِكَ الوَلَدُ	ذَانِكَ+الوَلَدَان=ذَانِكَ الوَلَدَان	أُولَئِكَ+ الأَوْلَادُ= أُولَئِكَ الأَوْلَادُ

So, the meaning of (ذَالِكَ الوَلَدُ) will be "That boy" in singular case whereas the meaning of (ذَانِكَ الوَلَدَان) will be "Those two boys". As far as the Plural case is concerned, it will mean "Those boys".

Example (2) (b) :

Feminine Singular	Feminine Dual	Feminine Plural
تِلكَ+المَرْاَةُ=تِلكَ المَرْاَةُ	تَانِكَ+المَرْأتَانِ=تَانِكَ المَرْأتَانِ	أُولٰئِكَ+النِّسَاءُ=أُولٰئِكَ النِّسَاءُ

Just like the Masculine, the Singular of Feminine (تِلكَ المَرْأةُ) means "That woman" and the Dual of it (تَانِكَ المَرْأتَانِ) means "Those two women" and the Plural form (أُولٰئِكَ النِّسَاءُ) gives the meaning as "Those women".

Things to remember:

*Demonstrative Pronouns of English i.e. "This" and "That" have their equivalents in Arabic and they are called "Ismul-isha-ra-tu" (إِسْمُ الإِشَارَةِ)
.

*Demonstrative Pronoun or (إِسْمُ الإِشَارَةِ) is prefixed to a noun. Any such noun following immediately after (إِسْمُ الإِشَارَةِ)is called (المُشَارُإِلَيْهِ)"Al-mu-sha-ru i-lai-hi".

*Demonstrative Pronoun is prefixed to a definite noun as given in the examples. However,a Demonstrative Pronoun prefixed to an indefinite noun is called Subject and the noun followed by it is called Predicate. Example: هَذَا وَلَدٌ (This is a boy) .

Note: You will know about "Subject and Predicate" in the next chapter.

Read loudly and Practice

1. ذَالِكَ المِنْدِيْلُ (That handkerchief)
2. تِلكَ السَّيَّارَةُ (That car)
3. هَؤُلَاءِ البَنَا تُ (These girls)
4. هٰذَانِ اللَّاعِبَانِ (These two players)
5. ذَانِكَ السَّائِقَانِ (Those two drivers)
6. هٰذَالشَّا رِعُ (This street)
7. أُولٰئِكَ التُّجَّارُ (Those businessmen)
8. تَانِكَ الفَتَا تَانِ (Those two young girls)

Chapter 7
Subject and Predicate

If you want to say in your daily conversation that:

- The classroom is small
- The tea is cold
- The weather is hot

How will you say these things in Arabic? In this Chapter you will know how to express such things. Look at the examples given in the below column:

The Subject and Predicate	المُبْتَدَأ وَالخَبَرُ
The classroom is small The tea is cold The weather is hot The boy is big The girl is small	الفَصْلُ صَغِيْرٌ الشَّايُ+ بَارِدٌ = الشَّايُ بَارِدُ الطَّقسُ+حَارٌّ = الطَّقسُ حَارٌّ الوَلَدُ+ كَبِيْرٌ = الوَلَدُ كَبِيْرٌ البِنْتُ+ صَغِيْرَةٌ = البِنْتُ صَغِيْرَةٌ

Just by looking at the above examples you can understand that "subject and predicate" consist of two nouns. A definite noun (الفَصْلُ) and an indefinite noun (صَغِيْرٌ) .

The structure of the sentence is such that the definite noun comes first and then comes the indefinite noun.

The definite noun which comes first is called "Subject" or (المُبْتَدَأ)and the indefinite noun followed by it is called "Predicate" or الخَبَرُ.

The subject carries vowel mark "Damma" and the predicate carries vowel mark "Damma with nunation".

The structure of a sentence formed with subject and predicate is as below:

Subject and predicate	المُبْتَدَأ + الخَبَرُ = المُبْتَدَأ وَالخَبَرُ
The street is crowded	الشَّارِعُ + مُزْدَحِمٌ = الشَّا رِ عُ مُزْدَحِمٌ

Keeping this pattern in mind try to understand the following examples of "The subject and predicate":

The room is closed.	الغُرْفَةُ مُغْلَقَةٌ
The car is parked.	السَيَّا رَةُ وَاقِفَةٌ
The driver is asleep.	السَّا ئِقُ نَا ئِمٌ
The chair is broken.	الكُرْسِيُّ مَكْسُوْرٌ
The cook is expert.	الطَّبَّا خُ مَا هِرٌ
This is a book.	هَذَا كِتَا بٌ
That is a notebook.	تِلكَ كُرَّاسَةٌ

Things to remember

(1) If Subject (اَلمُبْتَدَأ)is singular then the predicate (اَلخَبَرُ)will also be singular.

Likewise, if subject (اَلمُبْتَدَأ)is dual or plural then the predicate (اَلخَبَرُ) will be brought as dual or plural as well.

Examples:

The house is spacious المَنْزِلُ وَاسِعٌ. (Singular subject and predicate)

The two pens are new القَلمَانِ جَدِيْدَانِ. (Dual subject and plural)

The men are asleep الرِّجَا لُ نَائِمُوْنَ. (Plural subject and predicate)

(2) If subject (اَلمُبْتَدَأ)is masculine then the predicate (اَلخَبَرُ)will also be masculine.

Example:

The shirt is expensive اَلقَمِيْصُ ثَمِيْنٌ

(3) If the subject (اَلمُبْتَدَأ)is feminine then the predicate (اَلخَبَرُ)will also be feminine.

Example:

The girl is beautiful الفَتَاةُ جَمِيْلَةٌ

Read out loudly:

The air is clean.	الهواءُ نَظِيْفٌ
The season is good.	المَوْسِمِ جَيِّدٌ
The sky is clear.	السَّمَاءُ صَافٍ
The patient is thin.	المَرِيْضُ نَحِيفٌ
The doctor is fat.	الطَّبِيْبُ سَمِيْنٌ
The school is near by.	المَدْرَسَةُ قرِيْبَةٌ
The dog is hungry.	الكَلبُ جَائِعٌ

Vocabulary:

The woman	المَرْأةُ \ النِّسَاءُ
The President	الرَّئِيسُ \ الرُّؤُوْسَاءُ
Expensive	ثَمِيْنٌ
Cheap	رَخِيْصٌ
Table	طَا وِلَة \ طَا وِلَاتٌ
Desk	مِنْضَدَةٌ \ مَنَاضِدُ
Refrigerator	ثَلَاجَة \ ثَلَاجَاتٌ
Cloth	ثَوْبٌ \ ثِيَابٌ
Needy	فَقِيْرٌ \ فُقَرَاءُ
Empty	خَالِيَةٌ
Ignorant/illiterate	جَاهِلٌ
Hungry	جَائِعٌ
Nearby	قَرِيْبٌ
Faraway	بَعِيْدٌ
Clean	نَظِيْفٌ

Exercise-1

Fill in the blanks with suitable predicate:

1. ....الطَّبِيْبُ
2. ....الكُرْسِيُّ
3. ....الغُرْفَةُ
4. ....الكِتَابُ
5. ....المَرْأةُ
6. ....الرَّئِيس

Hints: خَطِيْبٌ (an orator) , خَجُوْلَةٌ (Shy) , كَبِيْرَةٌ (big) , مَكْسُوْرٌ (broken) , مَفْتُوْحٌ (open) , مَشْغُوْلٌ (busy) .

Exercise-2

Fill in the blank with suitable subject:

1. كَبِيْرَةٌ............
2. نَائِمٌ............
3. فَقِيْرٌ.............
4. جَاهِلٌ..............
5. صَغِيْرَةٌ..............
6. خَالِيَةٌ...............

Hints: الأَبُ (The father) , القَاعَةُ (The hall) , الغَرِيْبُ (The stranger) , البُسْتَانِيُّ (The gardener) , المِنَصَّةُ (The stage) , المَدِيْنَةُ (The City) .

Chapter 8
The Noun Qualified and the Adjective

For expressions like "the new student", "a beautiful girl" and "the fresh air" the following pattern is followed in Arabic:

The Noun Qualified and the adjective	الْمَوْصُوْفُ وَالصِّفَةُ
A new student	طَالِبٌ + جَدِيْدٌ = طَا لِبٌ جَدِيْدٌ
The beautiful girl	اَلْفَتَاةُ + الْجَمِيْلَةُ = اَلْفَتَاةُ الْجَمِيْلَةُ
The fresh air	اَلْهَوَاءُ + النَّقِيُّ = اَلْهَوَاءُ النَّقِيُّ

The first noun is called (noun qualified) or اَلْمَوْصُوْفُ and the second noun is called (adjective) or الصِّفَةُ.

You can understand from the above given examples that the noun qualified and the adjective consist of two nouns. Both of them can either be indefinite or definite. Look at some more examples for further clarification:

	الْمَوْصُوْفُ وَ الصِّفَةُ
The new student	اَلطَّالِبُ الْجَدِيْدُ
The old school	اَلْمَدْرَسَةُ الْقَدِيْمَةُ
The shining notebook	اَلدَّفْتَرُ اللَّامِعُ
The beautiful office	اَلْمَكْتَبُ الْجَمِيْلُ
The expert engineer	اَلْمُهَنْدِسُ الْمَاهِرُ
The successful businessman	اَلتَّاجِرُ النَّاجِحُ
The fresh fruit	اَلْفَاكِهَةُ الطَّازِجَةُ
A narrow street	شَارِعٌ ضَيِّقٌ
A broken car	سَيَّارَةٌ مَكْسُوْرَةٌ

A dirty child	طِفْلٌ وَسِخٌ
The closed door	اَلبَابُ المُغْلَقُ
The open road	الطَّرِيْقُ المَفْتُوْحُ

As it is apparent from the above mentioned examples that each sentence is made of two nouns. First of these two is called "Noun qualified" or (المَوْصُوْفُ)and the second one is called "Adjective" or (الصِّفَةُ).

In English, the adjective comes first and then comes the noun qualified. However, in Arabic the reverse is true as the noun qualified comes first and then comes the adjective as you can understand it well by looking at the sample sentences of both the languages. But to make it more clear, a structural analysis is being given in the following column:

Adjective + Noun	المَوْصُوْفُ + الصِّفَةُ
The visiting + Professor	الأُسْتَاذُ + الزَّائِرُ

So, you can see that the order of the Arabic sentence got reversed in the English one.

You must be aware that a noun qualified or المَوْصُوْفُ can have more than one adjective or الصِّفَةُ. So, if a noun qualified (المَوْصُوْفُ)has more than one adjective (الصِّفَةُ)then all the adjectives can be written after the noun qualified in the following order:

(الطَّرِيْقُ + الطَّوِيْلُ +الشَّاقُ + المُجْهِدُ = الطَّرِيْقُ الطَّوِيْلُ الشَّاقُ المُجْهِدُ)

(The long, difficult and tiring road)

Things to remember:

*Noun qualified and adjective have to be compatible with each other in the following four things:

(1) Both will carry the same vowel mark on their last letters.

Example:

الطَّالِبُ الجَدِيْدُ "Damma" in case of nominative case.

الطَّالِبَ الجَدِيْدَ "Fatha" in case of accusative case.

الطَّالِبِ الجَدِيْدِ "Kasra" in case of genitive case.

(2) Both, the noun and the adjective, have to be of the same gender. **Example:**
   (a) اَلأُسْتَاذُ الْكَرِيْمُ (The kind teacher) both are masculine.
   (b) الطَّالِبَةُ الذَّكِيَّةُ (The intelligent female student) both are feminine.

(3) If the noun is singular then the adjective will be singular as well. The same will be true for dual and plural as well. **Example:**
   (a) الزَّعِيمُ الصَّادِقُ (The honest leader) both are singular.
   (b) الزَّعِيْمَانِ الصَّادِقَانِ (The two honest leaders) both are dual.
   (c) الزُّعَمَاءُ الصَّادِقُوْنَ (The honest leaders) both are plural.

(4) Both will be either definite or indefinite. Example:
   (a) الطَّالِبُ الْجَدِيْدُ (The new student) both are definite.
   (b) طَالِبٌ جَدِيْدٌ (A new student) both are indefinite.

NOTE:

If the noun qualified is non-sensible plural then the adjective will always be singular and feminine. Example:

اَلْأَبْوَابُ الْمُغْلَقَةُ (The closed doors)

اَلْأَشْيَاءُ الْمَكْسُوْرَةُ (The broken things)

Here in the above examples, اَلْأَبْوَابُ and اَلْأَشْيَاءُ are non-sensible plural nouns whose adjective الْمُغْلَقَةُ and الْمَكْسُوْرَةُ have been brought as singular feminine.

Vocabulary

New	جَدِيْدٌ
Old	قَدِيْمٌ
Notebook	دَفْتَرٌ\دَفَاتِرُ
Shining	لَامِعٌ
Office	مَكْتَبٌ\مَكَاتِبُ
Beautiful	جَمِيْلٌ
Engineer	مُهَنْدِسٌ\مُهَنْدِسُوْنَ
Expert	مَاهِرٌ\مَاهِرُوْنَ
Businessman	تَاجِرٌ\تُجَّارٌ
Successful	نَاجِحٌ\نَاجِحُوْنَ
Fruit	فَاكِهَةٌ\فَوَاكِهُ

Fresh	طَازِجٌ
Street	شَارِعٌ\شَوَارِعُ
Narrow	ضَيِّقٌ
Car	سَيَّارَةٌ\سَيَّارَاتٌ
Broken	مَكْسُورَةٌ\مَكْسُورَاتٌ
Open	مَفْتُوْحٌ
Child	طِفْلٌ\أطْفَالٌ
Dirty	وَسِخٌ
Road	طَرِيْقٌ\طُرُقٌ
Door	بَابٌ\أبْوَابٌ
Closed	مُغْلَقٌ

Chapter 9
How to use (OF) and ('S)

To express possession in English you either use (of) or apostrophic ('s) and the sentence is formed as below:
The book of Hamid
The watch of Sara
So, if you look at the above sentences it can be divided into two parts:

- Part one is about what is possessed.
- Part two is about who possesses it.

Now, look at the below given Arabic sentences:

Demonstration of possession	المُضافُ وَالمُضافُ اِلَيْهِ
The book of Hamid	كِتَابُ حَامِدٍ
Khalid's watch	سَاعَةُ خَالِدٍ
The house of a businessman	مَنْزِلُ تَاجِرٍ
The friend of the farmer	صَدِيْقُ الفَلاَّحِ
The Chief of the Municipality	عَمِيْدُ البَلَدِيَّةِ
The window of the room	شُبَّاكُ الغُرْفَةِ
The bag of the father	حَقِيْبَةُ الأَبِ

You can understand it very well now. Part of the sentence coming before (of) and showing what is possessed is called (المُضَافُ)and the other part of the sentence coming after (of) and showing who possesses it is called (المُضَافُ اِلَيْهِ).
المُضَافُ (Al-mu-dha-fu) denotes what is possessed whereas المُضَافُ اِلَيْهِ (Al-mu-dha-fu ilai-hi) indicates the possessor.
Structure of the sentence would be:

Demonstration of possession	المُضَافُ + المُضَافُ اِلَيْهِ
The bicycle of the student The friend of Khalid	دَرَّاجَةُ + الطَّالِبِ = دَرَّاجَةُ الطَّالِبِ صَدِيْقُ + خَالِدٍ = صَدِيْقُ خَالِدٍ

اَلْمُضَافُ cannot carry tanween (Nunation) or definite article (اَلْ) however, (Al-mudhaf) is still considered as definite because it indicates possession to a particular person or thing.

The vowel mark of (اَلْمُضَافُ)can be either of the three vowel marks i.e. "damma", "fat-ha" and "kasra" depending on the situation but it can never carry tanween (nunation) .

Vowel mark of (اَلْمُضَافُ اِلَيْهِ)will always be "kasra" including "nunation" except when (اَلْمُضَافُ اِلَيْهِ)happens to be a definite proper noun which does not accept "kasra" or "nunation" on its last letter. In such a case "kasra" or "kasra with nunation" will be replaced with "fat-ha". Such definite proper nouns are:

مَرْيَمُ ,خَدِيْجَةُ ,حَفْصَةُ ,زَيْنَبُ ,فَاطِمَةُ etc.

اَلْمُضَافُ اِلَيْهِ can also carry definite article (اَلْ)as and when need arises.

If (اَلْمُضَافُ)is dual noun then the last letter of it i.e. (ن) will be dropped. Thus the sentence will be as below:

صَدِيْقَا الْمُعَلِّمِ (The two friends of the teacher) in nominative case.

And صَدِيْقَيْ الْمُعَلِّمِ in accusative and genitive cases

In the same manner, if (اَلْمُضَافُ)is a plural noun made by adding (وْنَ) then the (نَ)will be replaced with (ا)as in مُسْلِمُوْا الْهِنْدِ (The Muslims of India) in nominative case and the وَاوُ of plural will be replaced with ي in accusative and genitive cases as in مُسْلِمِي الْهِنْدِ.

The adjective of اَلْمُضَافُ is always brought after اَلْمُضَافُ اِلَيْهِ. Example: قَمِيْصُ الْأَبِ الْجَدِيْدُ (Father's new shirt) . Here, اَلْجَدِيْدُ is adjective of اَلْمُضَافُ which is قَمِيْصُ but it has been brought after اَلْمُضَافُ اِلَيْهِ that is اَلْأَبِ.

But if you want to form a sentence as per the rule of subject (اَلْمُبْتَدَأُ) and predicate (اَلْخَبَرُ)then Al-mudha-fu (اَلْمُضَافُ)and Al-mudha-fu ilai-hi (اَلْمُضَافُ اِلَيْهِ)together will form as subject (اَلْمُبْتَدَأُ)and a separate noun will be brought as predicate (اَلْخَبَرُ)which has to be compatible with Al-mudha-fu (اَلْمُضَافُ)in gender and number. Look at the below examples:

Meaning	اَلْمُضَا فُ+ اَلْمُضَافُ اِلَيْهِ = اَلْمُبْتَدَأُ+اَلْخَبَرُ
The pen of Khalid is new.	قَلَمُ خَالِدٍ جَدِيْدٌ
The watch of Mary is expensive.	سَاعَةُ مَرْيَمَ ثَمِيْنَةٌ
The car of Gandhi is fast.	سَيَّارَةُ غَانْدِيْ سَرِيْعَةٌ
The director of the co. is tall.	مُدِيْرُ الشَّرِكَةِ طَوِيْلٌ

The two boys of the school are standing.	وَلَدَا المَدْرَسَةِ وَاقِفَان
The men of village are strong.	رِجَالُ القَرْيَةِ أقوِيَاءُ

Personal pronoun as المُضَافُ اِلَيْهِ

In the previous pages you observed examples where a noun was used as المُضَافُ اِلَيْهِ. Now, you must know about certain other examples where the personal pronouns are used as المُضَافُ اِلَيْهِ.

But before you proceed any further you should know what those personal pronouns are in Arabic? Personal pronouns in Arabic are known as ضَمَائِرٌ\ضمِيْرٌ (Dha-maa-iru) . These are as under:

Masculine	Feminine	Masculine	Feminine
هُوَ He (s)	هِيَ She (s)	أنْتَ You (s)	أنْتِ You (s)
هُمَا Those (d)	هُمَا Those (d)	أنْتُمَا You (d)	أنْتُمَا You (d)
هُمْ They (p)	هُنَّ They (p)	أنْتُمْ You (p)	أنْتُنَّ You (p)

Now at look at the below examples also so you can have a proper understanding of the personal pronouns (ضَمَائِرُ).

(a) :

Masculine	Feminine
بَيْتُهُ His house (s)	بَيْتُهَا Her house (s)
بَيْتُهُمَا Their houses (d)	بَيْتُهُمَا Their houses (d)
بَيْتُهُمْ Their houses (p)	بَيْتُهُنَّ Their houses (p)

(b) :

Masculine	Feminine
بَيْتُكَ Your house (s)	بَيْتُكِ Your house (s)
بَيْتُكُمَا Your houses (d)	بَيْتُكُمَا Your houses (d)
بَيْتُكُمْ Your houses (p)	بَيْتُكُنَّ Your houses (p)

See the examples in columns (a) and (b) . Here, the personal pronouns have been used as (الْمُضَافُ اِلَيْهِ) .

You should also remember that there are two kinds of personal pronouns.

1. One of them always comes attached to a noun as in the below given examples and such personal pronouns are called ضَمِيْرٌ مُتَّصِلٌ.

قَمِيْصُكَ Your shirt (MS)	حَقِيْبَتُكِ your bag (FS)
عَمُّهُ His uncle (MS)	بَيْتُكُمَا your houses (FD)
بَيْتُكُمْ Your houses (MP)	خِمَارُهُنَّ Their veils (FP)
قَلَمُكُمَا Your pens (MD)	عَمُّهَا Her uncle (FS)
خَالُهُمَا Their maternal uncle (MD)	أُخْتُكُنَّ Your sister (FP)

These personal pronouns also come attached with prepositions as in the below column:

لَهُ For him (MS)	لَهَا For her (FS)
لَهُمَا For them (MD)	لَهُمَا For them (FD)
لَهُمْ For them (MP)	لَهُنَّ Fir them (FP)
لَكَ For you (MS)	لَكِ For you (FS)
لَكُمَا For you (MD)	لَكُمَا For you (FD)
لَكُمْ For you (MP)	لَكُنَّ For you (FP)
لِيْ For me (MS/FS)	لِيْ For me (FS/MS)
لَنَا For us (MP/FP)	لَنَا For us (FP/MP)

2. There are another kind of personal pronouns which are used as detached from the noun and are called ضَمِيْرٌ مُنْفَصِلٌ. See the examples given below:
هُوَرَجُلٌ (He is a man) , هِيَ اِمْرَأَةٌ (she is a woman) , أَنْتَ كَرِيْمٌ (you are kind) , أَنَا طَالِبٌ (I am a student) , نَحْنُ مُعَلِّمُوْنَ (we are teachers) .

Note: Vowel marks (الإعْرَاب)of the personal pronouns do not change and remain inflexible in all the cases except in one case when (ه)is used along with a word whose last letter is either vowel-less or carries "kasra". **Example:**

عَلَيْهِ (on him) , اِلَيْهِ (towards him) , فِيْ بَيْتِهِ (in his house)

(You will know about prepositions in the following chapter in detail)

Vocabulary:

Sleeping	نَائِمٌ
Awake	يَقِظٌ
Tiring	مُجْهِدٌ
Colleague	زَمِيْلٌ
Room mate	زَمِيْلُ الغُرْفَةِ
A cow	بَقَرَةٌ
The buffalo	الجَامُوْسُ
A goat	خَرُوْفٌ
A bed	سَرِيْرٌ
A garden	حَدِيْقَةٌ

Exercise-1

Correct the following sentences:

بَيْتٌ حَامِدٌ

سَيَّارَةُ الْأُسْتَاذِ سَرِيْعٌ

كِتَابُ هُمَا جَدِيْدَةٌ

عُطُوْرُالهِنْدِ رَخِيْصٌ

اَلابْنُ المُدِيْر

Exercise-2

Translate the following sentences into Arabic.

1. The glass of water
2. The guard of the school

3. Mother's pillow
4. The father of the nation
5. The house of the doctor

Hints: زُجَاجٌ (a glass) , اَلْمَاءُ (the water) , حَارِسٌ (a guard) ,اَلْمَدْرَسَةُ (the school) ,وِسَادَةٌ (a pillow) , اَلْأُمُّ (the mother) , اَلْأَبُ (the father) , اَلْوَطَنُ (the nation) , بَيْتٌ (a house) , اَلطَّبِيْبُ (the doctor) .

Exercise-3

Fill in the blanks.

..........الطَّالِب وَسِخ

مِنْضَدَةُ الْأُسْتَاذِ.........

بَقَرَةُ حَامِدٍ.............

........الْمُهَنْدِس مُجْهَدٌ

زَمِيْلُ الْغُرْفَةِ..........

Hints: نَائِمٌ (sleeping) , عَمَلٌ (work) , سَمِيْنَةٌ (fat) , نَظِيْفَةٌ (clean) , قَمِيْصٌ (shirt)

Chapter 10
Prepositions

Observe the following sentences:

From the house to the office	مِنَ الْبَيْتِ إِلَى الْمَكْتَبِ
In the car	بِالسَّيَّارَةِ
On the chair	عَلَى الْكُرْسِيِّ
In the hotel	فِيْ الْفُنْدُقِ
Like the criminal	كَالْمُجْرِمِ
For days	لِأَيَّامٍ
Since Saturday	مُنْذُ السَّبْتِ
Till noon	حَتَّى الظَّهِيْرَةِ
About the theft	عَنِ السَّرِقَةِ

I f you look at the above given examples closely you can realize that all the underlined words have given vowel mark "kasra" to all the nouns followed by it. These underlined words are called prepositions or Hu-ru-ful Jarre (حُرُوْفُ الجَرِّ) in Arabic.

A single "Preposition" is called har-ful-jar-re (حَرْفُ الجَرِّ)and the noun followed by is called (الْمَجْرُوْرُ)al-maj-ru-ru.

الْمَجْرُوْرُ (al-maj-ru-ru) has its fixed vowel mark as "kas-ra", however, there are few exceptions you will know about at a higher level of your understanding of Arabic grammar.

See some other examples as well which will be useful for you:

On the roof	فَوْقَ السَّقْفِ
Under the umbrella	تَحْتَ المِظَلَّةِ
In front of the teacher	قُدَّامَ الأُ سْتَاذِ
Before the leave/vacation	قَبْلَ العُطْلَةِ
Behind the wall	خَلفَ الجِدَارِ

After the meeting	بَعْدَ الإجْتِمَاع
Near the station	قُرْبَ المَحَطَّةِ
Beyond the river	وَرَاءَ النَّهْرِ
In front of the mosque	أمَامَ المَسْجِدِ

These underlined words are called Zu-ruful ma-kan (ظُرُوْفُ المَكَان)in Arabic or adverbs of place. Though these adverbs look like prepositions but they are not. These ظُرُوْفُ المَكَان always carry vowel mark "Fat-ha" on the last letter and are indeclinable as they never accept any other vowel mark.

Like المُضَافُ اِلَيْهِ or المَجْرُوْرُ, any noun followed by these adverbs receive vowel mark "kas-ra" as you can see in the examples above.

Chapter 11
Particles of Interrogation

Go through the model sentences below to know what are the interrogative particles (اَدَوَاتُ الإِسْتِفْهَام). These are used for asking questions and interrogation:

Interrogative particles	اَدَوَاتُ الإِسْتِفْهَام
Who are you?	مَنْ أنتَ؟
Where is your father?	أيْنَ أبُوْكَ؟
What is this?	مَا هَذَا؟
How do you do?	كَيْفَ حَالُكَ؟
Which pen do you want?	أيَّ قلمٍ تُرِيْدُ؟
Which woman is she?	أيَّةُ اِمْرَاَةٍ هِيَ؟
Why did you get delayed?	لِمَاذَا تَأَخَّرْتَ؟
When would you return?	مَتَى تَعُوْدُ؟
Is he a doctor?	هَلْ هُوَ طَبِيْبٌ؟
Did you eat?	أ أكَلْتَ؟

All the underlined words in the above model sentences of Arabic are called (اَدَوَاتُ الإِسْتِفْهَام)or interrogative particles. They do not influence the nouns followed by in any way and the vowel mark of these words or particles remain the same in every condition.

However, the word (أيٌّ)"ay-yu" and (أيَّةُ)"ay-ya-tu" are used as (المُضَافُ)"al-mu-dha-fu" hence the following noun gets vowel mark "kas-ra" for being (المُضَافُ اِلَيْهِ)"al-mu-dha-fu ilai-hi" as in (أيَّ قلمٍ تُرِيْدُ؟) and (أيَّةُ اِمْرَاَةٍ هِيَ؟)

(أيٌّ) is used with a masculine noun and (أيَّةُ)with feminine one. However, sometimes (أيٌّ)is used for both masculine and feminine noun.

Read the following conversation and practice the interrogative particles in daily life:

Who is that?	مَنْ ذَاكَ؟
He is a teacher.	هُوَ مُعَلِمٌ
Who are you?	مَنْ أنتَ؟
I am a doctor.	أنَا طَبِيْبٌ
How is the patient now?	كَيْفَ المَرِيْضُ الآنَ؟
He is in good health.	هُوَ فِيْ صِحَّةٍ جَيِّدَةٍ
What is in your hand?	مَا هُوَ بِيَدِكَ؟
This is my pen.	هَذَا قَلَمِيْ
Where is your friend?	أيْنَ صَدِيْقُكَ؟
He is in the car.	هُوَ فِيْ السَّيَّا رَةِ
When will you visit us again?	مَتَي تَزُوْرُنَا مَرَّةً أخْرَي؟
I will visit you very soon.	أزُوْرُكُمْ قَرِيْبَاَ جِدَّاً
In which hotel do you stay?	فِيْ أيِّ فُنْدُقٍ تَنْزِلُ؟
I am staying in hotel Taj.	أنَا نَزِيْلٌ فِيْ "التَّاج"
Is it a good place?	هَلْ هُوَ مَكَانٌ جَيِّدٌ؟
Of course.	طَبْعَاً
Bye.	مَعَ السَّلامَةِ

Exercise-1

Try to recognize the interrogative particles in the below sentences.

Do you eat apple?	هَلْ تَأ كُلُ التُّفَاحَ؟
What are these things?	مَا هَذِهِ الأشْيَاءُ؟
When do you sleep?	مَتَي تَنَامُ؟
Who entered my house?	مَنْ دَخَلَ فِيْ بَيْتِي؟
Where is your friend?	أيْنَ صَدِيْقُكَ؟
I do not know.	لا أعْلَمُ
Don,t you know?	ألا تَعْلَمُ ؟

He is your friend.	هُوَ صَدِيْقُكَ
How would I know?	كَيْفَ أَعْلَمُ؟
He is away from me.	هُوَ بَعِيْدٌ مِنِّي

Exercise-2

Translate these sentences into Arabic.

(1) Who is she?
(2) What is that?
(3) When do you leave?
(4) How is this room?
(5) Where is my bag?

Hints: تُغَادِرُ (you leave) , حَقِيْبَتِيْ (my bag) , أعْرف (I know) ,تَعْرِفُ (you know) ,تَنَامُ (You sleep) , دَخَلَ (entered) , بَيْتِيْ (my house) .

Chapter 12
The Particles of emphasis

You have already read about "subject and predicate" and the structure of a sentence based on this grammatical rule. However, look at the structure of the sentence once again:

Subject and predicate	اَلمُبْتَدأ وَ الخَبَرُ
The house is big	اَلبَيْتُ + كَبِيْرٌ= اَلبَيْتُ كَبِيْرٌ

Now look at some other sentences with "particles of emphasis" so that you can understand it well.

Indeed the house is big. But the school is small. It appears the child is playing. Perhaps the weather is bad.	اِنَّ البَيْتَ كَبِيْرٌ لكِنَّ المَدْرَسَةَ صَغِيْرَةٌ كَاَنَّ الطِّفْلَ لاَعِبٌ لَعَلَّ الطقسَ سَيِّءٌ

What difference did you find between the two sets of examples? You could see that (حُرُوْفُ التَّأكِيْدِ)or "particles of emphasis" made slight change in the meaning as well as the vowel mark of the first noun which comes immediately after the "particle". So, the structure of the sentence now becomes like this:

Particles of emphasis	أدَوَاتُ الإِسْتِفْهَام
Indeed the house is big. Perhaps the weather is bad.	اِنَّ + البَيْتَ + كَبِيْرٌ= اِنَّ البَيْتَ كَبِيْرٌ لعَلَّ+ الطَّقسَ+ سَيِّءٌ= لعَلَّ الطَّقسَ سَيِّءٌ

The "particle of emphasis" puts vowel mark "Fat-ha" or "Fat-ha with nunation" on the first noun -that is subject-which comes immediately after it and applies "Damma with nunation" on the predicate or the last noun.

If a "particle of emphasis" comes before a noun which has many adjectives then all such adjectives will get the vowel mark "Fat-ha" along with that particular noun like in:

لكِنَّ+ الطَّالِبَ الطَّوِيْلَ المُجْتَهِدَ الذَّكِيَّ+ نَائِمٌ = لكِنَّ الطَّالِبَ الطَّوِيْلَ المُجْتَهِدَ الذَّكِيَّ نَائِمٌ.

You can form sentences on the pattern given above by using different "particles of emphasis".

Read to practice:

The father is tall but the son is short.	الْأَبُ طَوِيْلٌ لكِنَّ الإِبْنَ قَصِيْرٌ
Who is the injured person?	مَنْ هُوَالشَّخْصُ الجَرِيْحُ؟
It seems he is your friend.	كَأنَّه صَدِيْقُكَ
Perhaps the doctor is late.	لعَلَّ الطَّبِيْبَ مُتَأَخِّرٌ
What is the shining thing?	مَا هُوَ الشَّئُ المُتَلَالأُ؟
It is a star.	إِنَّه نَجْمٌ

Vovabulary:

The son	الإِبْنُ
The daughter	البِنْتُ
The boy	الوَلَدُ
The wife	الزَّوْجَةُ
The husband	الزَّوْجُ
The father	الْأَبُ
The mother	الْأُمُّ
The brother	الْأَخُ
The sister	الْأُخْتُ
Your brother	اَخُوْكَ
Your sister	اُخْتُكَ
The big	الكَبِيْرُ

The small	الصَّغِيْرُ
The elder	الْأَكْبَرُ
The younger	الْأَصْغَرُ
The bench	الطَّاوِلَةُ
The desk	الْمِنْضَدَةُ
The new	الْجَدِيْدُ
The old	الْقَدِيْمُ
The park	الْحَدِيْقَةُ
The garden	الْبُسْتَانُ
The male child	الطِّفْلُ
The female child	الطِّفْلَةُ
The weather	الطَّقْسُ
Bad	سَيِّءٌ
Cold	بَارِدٌ
Hot	حَارٌّ
The summer	الصَّيْفُ
The winter	الشِّتَاءُ
The autumn	الْخَرِيْفُ
The spring	الرَّبِيْعُ
The wounded	الْجَرِيْحُ
The person	الشَّخْصُ
The director	الْمُدِيْرُ

Exercise-1

Fill in the blanks:

اِنَّ الْمَدْرَسَةَ قَرِيْبَةٌ..........الْبَنْكَ بَعِيْدٌ

..............الْمُدِيْر مَرِيْضٌ

........الْكِتَاب مَفْتُوْحٌ

الْقِطَّةُ بَاكِيَةٌ ......جَائِعَةٌ

......هُوَ الطَّالِبُ الْجَدِيْدُ؟

Exercise-2

Translate into Arabic:

(1) The Company is good but the director is bad.
(2) Who is your brother?
(3) What is in your pocket?
(4) Perhaps the weather is bad.
(5) Who is that boy?
(6) He seems to be your son.

Chapter 13
Conjugations of weak or (defective) verbs

Before you move ahead in your journey towards learning Arabic language you should memorize some conjugations given in the following columns. These are the conjugations of weak or defective verbs or اَلْأَفعَالُ النَاقِصَةُ and they are used along with noun as well as verbs. You will learn about their use bit later, first you should know about the conjugations:

(It means: was/were/ to be) (a) :

Imperative	Present/Future	Past
	يَكُوْنُ يَكُوْنَانِ يَكُوْنُوْنَ	كَانَ كَانَا كَا نُوْا
	تَكُوْنُ تَكُوْنَان يَكُنَّ	كَانَتْ كَانَتَا كُنَّ
كُنْ كُوْنَا كُوْنُوْا	تَكُوْنُ تَكُوْنَان تَكُوْنُوْنَ	كُنتَ كُنتُمَا كُنتُمْ
كُوْنِي كُوْنَا كُنَّ	تَكُوْنِيْنَ تَكُوْنَان تَكُنَّ	كُنتِ كُنتُمَا كُنتُنَّ
	أَكُوْنُ نَكُوْنُ	كُنْتُ كُنَّا

(b) :

Meaning	Past	Meaning	Past	Meaning	Past
To become	أَصْبَحَ أَصْبَحَا أَصْبَحُوْا	To become	صَارَ صَارَا صَارُوْا	Not to be	لَيْسَ لَيْسَا لَيْسُوْا
	أَصْبَحَتْ أَصْبَحَتَا أَصْبَحْنَ		صَارَتْ صَارَتَا صِرْنَ		لَيْسَتْ لَيْسَتَا لَسْنَ
	أَصْبَحْتَ أَصْبَحْتُمَا أَصْبَحْتُمْ		صِرْتَ صِرْتُمَا صِرْتُمْ		لَسْتَ لَسْتُمَا لَسْتُمْ
	أَصْبَحْتِ أَصْبَحْتُمَا أَصْبَحْتُنَّ		صِرْتِ صِرْتُمَا صِرْتُنَّ		لَسْتِ لَسْتُمَا لَسْتُنَّ
	أَصْبَحْتُ أَصْبَحْنَا		صِرْتُ صِرْنَا		لَسْتُ لَسْنَا

These are the conjugations of اَلْأَفْعَالُ النَّاقِصَةُ (Al-af-aa-lun-naqisa-tu) or weak verbs. They look like verbs and have conjugations just like verbs but they do not fulfill the task of a proper verb.

How to use them?

To have a better understanding with regards to their usage you have to recall the structure of "Subject and Predicate" (اَلْمُبْتَدَأُ وَالْخَبَرُ)once again. You have read about the structure of "the subject and the predicate" which was as below:

The house is small	اَلْبَيْتُ + صَغِيْرٌ = اَلْبَيْتُ صَغِيْرٌ

Now, if you want to say: "The house was big" then you will have to use (كَانَ)the weak verb or اَلْفِعْلُ النَّاقِصُ. Hence, the structure of the sentence will become as under:

The house was big	كَانَ + البَيْتُ + صَغِيْرًا= كَانَ البَيْتُ صَغِيْرًا

So you can understand that اَلْأفعَالُ النَّاقِصَةُ make certain changes in the structure of a sentence formed on the pattern of “subject and predicate”.

It gives “Damma” to the subject (المُبْتَدَأ)and “Fat-ha” or “Fat-ha with nunation” to the predicate (الخَبَرُ).

See some more examples to grasp the use of اَلْأفعَالُ النَّاقِصَةُ.

Incomplete verb+subject & predicate	اَلْأفعَالُ النَّاقِصَةُ+المُبْتَدَأ وَالخَبَرُ
The glass was full.	كَانَ الزُّجَاجُ مَلِيْئاً
The issue became easy.	أصْبَحَ الأمْرُ سَهْلاً
The room became big.	صَارَتِ الغُرْفَةُ كَبِيْرَةً
The nurse was tired	كَانَتِ المُمَرِّضَةُ تَعِبَةً
The question is not difficult.	لَيْسَ السُّؤَالُ صَعْباً\ بِصَعْبٍ
My friend became an engineer.	أصْبَحَ صَدِيْقِي مُهَنْدِساً
The two boys were criminals.	كَانَ الوَلَدَانِ مُجْرِمَيْنِ
The two girl students were laborious.	كَانَتِ الطَّالِبَتَانِ مُجْتَهِدَتَيْنِ
The men were business persons.	كَانَ الرِّجَالُ تُجَّاراً
The road is not paved.	لَيْسَ الطَّرِيْقُ مُعَبَّداً

You can see that اَلْأفعَالُ النَّاقِصَةُ have been brought before the “subject”. So if a subject is masculine then الفِعْلُ النَّاقِصُ will also be brought as masculine and will keep changing as per the gender.

Even when a “subject” (المُبْتَدَأ)is dual and plural “al-af-aa-lun-na-qisa-tu” (اَلْأفعَالُ النَّاقِصَةُ)remain singular.

However, if (اَلْأفعَالُ النَّاقِصَةُ)come between the subject (المُبْتَدَأ)and the predicate (الخَبَرُ)then the weak verb will be brought according to the subject. If subject is singular and masculine then (اَلْأفعَالُ النَّاقِصَةُ)will also be brought as per the subject and the same pattern will be followed for dual and plural cases. Look at some more examples in the following column:

The boy was sleeping.	الوَلَدُ كَانَ نَائِماً
The girl was sick.	البِنْتُ كَانَتْ مَرِيْضَة
The two boys were hungry.	الوَلَدَان كَانَا جَائِعَيْن
The two friends were nurses.	الصَّدِيْقَتَان كَانَتَا مُمَرِّضَتَيْن
The men were thieves.	الرِّجَالُ كَانُوْا لُصُوْصاً
The women were doctors.	النِّسَاءُ كُنَّ طَبِيْبَاتٍ

Vocabulary:

Sitting	جَالِسٌ
Standing	قَائِمٌ
Playing	لاعِبٌ
Beautiful	جَمِيْلٌ
The girl child	الطِّفْلَةُ
Happy	فَرِحٌ
Sad	حَزِيْنٌ
Hiding	مُخْتَفِيٌ
Busy with	مَشْغُوْلٌ ب
The study	الدِّرَاسَةُ

Exercise-1

Correct the sentences in the below given examples:

كَانَ المُدَرِّسُ جَالِسٌ فِي الغُرْفَةِ

الأوْلادُ كَانَ لاعِبِيْنَ

كَانَتِ الخَادِمَةُ غَائِبًا

النِّسَاءُ كَانَتْ نَائِمَة

صَارَتِ البَيْتُ جَمِيْلا

أصْبَحَتِ الطِّفْلَةُ فَرِحاً

Exercise-2

Fill in the blank:

........أبيْ مَرِيْضاً وَ كُنْتُ ....

أصْبَحَتِ الطَّبِيْبَةُ ....

............اللُصُوْصُ مُخْتَفِيْنَ فِي الغَابَةِ

المُدَرِّسَة ....جَالِسَةَ فِي الغُرْفَةِ

الطُّلاَّبُ . .... مَشْغُوْلِيْنَ بِالدِّرَاسَةِ

Hints: كَانَ ,مُتَأَخِّرَة ,جَائِعاً ,كَانَتْ ,كَانُوْا

Chapter 14
Kinds of sentence

As you are going to start a chapter on verb (اَلفِعْلُ)in the following pages, it is essential to know how many kinds of sentences are there in Arabic language.

There are two kinds of sentences in Arabic:

(1) Nominal sentences (اَلجُمَلُ الإِسْمِيَّةُ)

(2) Verbal sentences (اَلجُمَلُ الفِعْلِيَةُ)

A sentence which starts with a noun (اَلإِسْمُ)is called "nominal sentence" or (اَلجُمْلَةُ الإِسْمِيَّةُ).

Examples are:

The factory is big.	اَلمَصْنَعُ كَبِيْرٌ
The market of Delhi is famous.	سُوْقُ دِهْلِيْ شَهِيْرَةٌ
Policemen are sitting.	رِجَالُ الشُّرْطَةِ جَالِسُوْنَ

Likewise, a sentence which starts with a verb (اَلفِعْلُ)is called verbal sentence or (اَلجُمْلَةُ الفِعْلِيَةُ).

Example are:

The father drank tea.	شَرِبَ الْأَبُ الشَّايَ
The guest checked in the hotel.	نَزَلَ الضَّيْفُ فِي الفُنْدُق
The mother cooked food.	طَبَخَتِ الْأُمُّ الطَّعَامَ

Till now you have read about the nominal sentences in the previous chapters. From here onwards you will read and understand how a verbal sentence is formed in the following chapters.

Past, Present and Future:

Like English, verb in Arabic also has three tenses:

(1) Past
(2) Present and
(3) Future

The Past is called "Al-fe'lul-madhi" (الفِعْلُ المَاضِي)however, present and future tenses in Arabic are known with a single name i.e. "Al-fe'lul-mudha-reu" (الفِعْلُ المُضَارِعُ).

The chapters in this book will deal with Past tense or (الفِعْلُ المَاضِي)first and then you will move to Present and Future tenses.

Chapter 15
The Past Tense

Before dealing with model sentences and examples based on Past tense it is appropriate to know few basic things about the verbs whether past, present or future.

A verb can be trilateral or can even consist of four letters or more than that but its root is ف ع ل. Majority of the verbs are trilateral but there are verbs with more than three letters about which you will know as you develop your skill to learn this language.

The verbs are further devided into transitive (اَلفِعْلُ المُتَعَدِّيْ)and intransitive (اَلفِعْلُ اللّازِمُ).

Transitive verb (اَلفِعْلُ المُتَعَدِّيْ)requires both "doer" and "object" for completion of a sentence:

Subject + verb + object	اَلفِعْلُ + اَلفَاعِلُ + اَلمَفْعُوْلُ
The children drank water	شَرِبَ الْأَطْفَالُ المَاءَ

Intransitive verb (اَلفِعْلُ اللّازِمُ)does not require an object for completing a sentence:

Subject + verb	اَلفِعْلُ + اَلفَاعِلُ
The teacher sat. The servant went.	جَلَسَ المُعَلِّمُ ذَهَبَ الخَادِمُ

Both Past and Present/Future tenses have fourteen patterns of conjugation which are being given in the following column. You must memorize them for effective result.

The conjugation of Past tense	تَصْرِيْفُ الفِعْلِ المَاضِي
He Did (MS) They did (MD) They did (MP)	فَعَلَ فَعَلَا فَعَلُوْا

She did (FS)	فَعَلَتْ
They did (FD)	فَعَلَتَا
They did (FP)	فَعَلْنَ
You did (MS)	فَعَلْتَ
You did (MD)	فَعَلْتُمَا
You did (MP)	فَعَلْتُمْ
You did (FS)	فَعَلْتِ
You did (FD)	فَعَلْتُمَا
You did (SP)	فَعَلْتُنَّ
I did (M/F)	فَعَلْتُ
We did (M/F)	فَعَلْنَا

Now look at the below given conversation in the column where past tense has been used in different situations:

The guest came from Delhi.	جَاءَ الضَّيْفُ مِنْ مَدِيْنَةِ دِهْلِي
And reached our home.	وَ وَصَلَ اِلي بَيْتِنَا
We requested him to enter the room.	طَلَبْنَاه الدُّخُوْلَ فِي الْغُرْفَةِ
The two servants also entered with him.	دَخَلَ الخَادِمَانِ مَعَهُ أَيْضاً
The guest sat on the chair.	جَلَسَ الضَّيْفُ عَلَي الْكُرْسِيِّ
And the servants sat on the bed.	وَ جَلَسَ الْخَادِمَانِ عَلَي السَّرِيْرِ
The guest ate the food.	أَكَلَ الضَّيْفُ الطَّعَامَ
As far as the servants are concerned, they ate sweets.	أَمَّا الخَادِمَانِ فَأَكَلاَ الحَلْوَي
My mother entered the room.	دَخَلَتْ أُمِّي الْغُرْفَة
And greeted the guest.	وَ سَلَّمَتْ عَلَي الضَّيْفِ
Khalid, Hamid and Majid also	جَاءَ خَالِدٌ وَ حَامِدٌ وَمَاجِدٌ أَيْضاً

came.	
They greeted the guest.	وَسَلَمُوْا عَلَيْ الضَّيْفِ
And they sat in front of him.	وَجَلَسُوْا أَمَامَهُ
Sadiqa and Rafea took permission to enter.	طَلَبَتْ "صَادِقَةُ" وَ "رَافِعَةُ" اَلِإذْنَ بِالدُّخُوْلِ
And their friends also took permission.	وَصَدِيقَاتُهَا طَلَبْنَ الإذْنَ أَيْضاً
Then my father returned from the office in the evening.	ثُمَّ رَجَعَ أَبِيْ مِنَ المَكْتَبِ فِي المَسَاءِ
And visited the guest after some time.	وَزَارَ الضَّيْفَ بَعْدَ مُرُوْرِ وَقْتٍ
Asked about the journey and his conditions.	وَ سَأَلَهُ عَنِ السَّفَرِوَ أَحْوَالِهِ
And asked him also:	وَ سَأَلَه أَيْضاً:
Did you eat food?	هَلْ أَكَلْتَ الطَّعَامَ؟
Yes, I ate?	نَعَمْ, أَكَلْتُ
The guest replied.	أَجَا بَ الضَّيْفُ
And did both of you eat?	وَهَلْ أَكَلْتُمَا؟
My father asked the servants.	سَأَلَ أَبِيْ الخَادِمَيْنِ
Yes, we also ate, they replied.	نَعَمْ, أَكَلْنَا أَيْضاً, أَجَابَ الخَادِمَانِ
Then we came out of the room.	ثُمَّ خَرَجْنَا مِنَ الغُرْفَةِ
And we left the guest so he can rest	وَ تَرَكْنَا الضَّيْفَ لِيَسْتَرِيْحَ

(a) If the subject (الفَاعِلُ)is masculine then the verb will also be brought as masculine:

The guest ate the food.	أَكَلَ الضَّيْفُ الطَّعَامَ

Here, (أَكَلَ)a masculine verb has been used because the subject (الفَاعِلُ)is a masculine noun which is (الضَّيْفُ).

(b) If the subject is a feminine noun then a feminine verb will be used:

The mother entered the room.	دَخَلتِ الأمُّ الغُرْفة

The verb (دَخَلتْ)here has been brought as feminine because the subject (اَلْأمُّ)is a feminine noun.

(c) The verb (اَلفِعْلُ)will always remain singular no matter whether a subject (اَلفَاعِلُ)is brought as singular, dual or plural if the above structure is followed. See the below examples as well for further clarification:

The man came.	جَاءَ الرَّجُلُ
The two men came.	جَاءَ الرَّجُلَانْ
The men came.	جَاءَ الرِّجَالُ

However, if the structure of the sentence is changed as it starts with a noun, in that case the verb (اَلفِعْلُ)will be brought as per the subject (اَلفَاعِلُ). If the subject is singular, dual or plural the verb will also follow suit:

The guest ate the food.	اَلضَّيْفُ أكَلَ الطَّعَامَ
The two guests ate the food.	اَلضَّيْفَانِ أكَلاَ الطَّعَامَ
The guests ate the food.	اَلضُّيُوْفُ أكَلُوْا الطَّعَامَ

Vocabulary:

The guest	اَلضَّيْفُ\الضُّيُوْفُ
A city	مَدِيْنَةٌ\ مُدُنٌ
To reach	وَصَلَ\يَصِلُ\وُصُوْلاً
To request/ to demand	طلبَ\يَطْلُبُ\طلباً
Entering	اَلدُّخُوْلُ
To enter	دَخَلَ\يَدْخُلُ\دُخُوْلاً
A room	غُرْفَةٌ\غُرَفٌ

The servant	الخَادِمُ\الخُدَّامُ
The bed	السَّرِيْرُ\الأسِرَّةُ
To eat	أكَلَ\يَأكُلُ\أكْلاً
To sit	جَلَسَ\يَجْلِسُ\جُلُوْساً
The chair	الكُرْسِيُّ\الكَرَاسِيُّ
The food	الطَّعَامُ\الأطْعِمَةُ
The sweets	الحَلوَي\ الحَلاوَي
To greet	سَلَّمَ\يُسَلِّمُ\تَسْلِيْمَاً عَلَي
To come	جَاءَ \ يَجِيءُ \مَجِيْئاً
Permission	الإِذْنُ
Female friend	صَدِيْقَةٌ\ صَدِيْقَاتٌ
To return	رَجَعَ \ يَرْجِعُ\ رُجُوْعاً
The office	المَكْتَبُ \ المَكَاتِبُ
To visit	زَارَ \ يَزُوْرُ \ زِيَارَةً
Time	وَقْتٌ \ أوْقَاتٌ
Passage	مُرُوْرٌ
To ask	سَألَ \ يَسْألُ \ سُؤَالاً
Yes	نَعْمْ
To respond/ to reply	أجَابَ \ يُجِيْبُ \اِجَابَةً
To come out	خَرَجَ \ يَخْرُجُ \خُرُوْجاً
To leave	تَرَكَ \ يَتْرُكُ \تَرْكاً
To take rest	اِسْتَرَاحَ \ يَسْتَرِيْحُ \ اِسْتَرَاحاً

Conjugations

Conjugations of two more verbs are being given in the following column. Memorize them for use in day-to-day conversation.

Meaning	الفِعْلُ المَاضِي	الضَّمَائِرُ	Meaning	الفِعْلُ المَاضِي	الضَّمَائِرُ
He entered	دَخَلَ	هُوَ	He ate	أكَلَ	هُوَ
They entered	دَخَلَا	هُمَا	They ate	أكَلَا	هُمَا
They entered	دَخَلُوْا	هُمْ	They ate	أكَلُوْا	هُمْ
She entered	دَخَلَتْ	هِيَ	She ate	أكَلَتْ	هِيَ
They entered	دَخَلَتَا	هُمَا	They ate	أكَلَتَا	هُمَا
They entered	دَخَلْنَ	هُنَّ	They ate	أكَلْنَ	هُنَّ
You entered	دَخَلْتَ	أنْتَ	You ate	أكَلْتَ	أنْتَ
You entered	دَخَلْتُمَا	أنْتُمَا	You ate	أكَلْتُمَا	أنْتُمَا
You entered	دَخَلْتُمْ	أنْتُمْ	You ate	أكَلْتُمْ	أنْتُمْ
You entered	دَخَلْتِ	أنْتِ	You ate	أكَلْتِ	أنْتِ
You entered	دَخَلْتُمَا	أنْتُمَا	You ate	أكَلْتُمَا	أنْتُمَا
You entered	دَخَلْتُنَّ	أنْتُنَّ	You ate	أكَلْتُنَّ	أنْتُنَّ
I entered	دَخَلْتُ	أنَا	I ate	أكَلْتُ	أنَا
We entered	دَخَلْنَا	نَحْنُ	We ate	أكَلْنَا	نَحْنُ

Exercise-1

Complete the conjugation of the following verbs on the pattern given in the above column:
صَدَقَ, (he spoke truth) نَصَرَ, (he helped) , جَلَسَ (he sat) .

Exercise-2

Translate into English:

نَامَ الطِّفْلُ عَلي السَّرِيْر
وَقَفَتِ السَّيَّارَةُ أمَامَ البَيْتِ
جَلَسَ المُسَافِرُوْنَ عَلي المَقَاعِدِ
الطُّلَّابُ دَرَسُوْا الأسْبَاقَ
مَدَّ المَرِيْضُ رِجْلَهُ

Hints: نَامَ, (he slept) السَّرِيْرُ (the bed) , وَقَفَتْ (stood) , اَلْمُسَافِرُوْنَ (travelers) , اَلمَقَاعِدُ (the seats) , دَرَسُوْا (they studied) , اَلْأَسْبَاق (the lessons) ,مَدَّ (he spread) , رِجْلَهُ (his leg) .

Exercise-3

Fill in the blanks:

.......الْأُسْتَاذُ مِنَ الغُرْفَةِ

اَلْبَنَاتُ ....الطَّعَامَ

......الْأَقْرِبَاءُ المَرِيْضَ

Hints: خَرَجَ (He came out) , طَبَخْنَ (they cooked) , زَارَ (visited)

Chapter 16
Present and Future Tense

Like the past tense (الفِعلُ المَاضِي)Present/Future tense (الفِعلُ المُضَارِعُ) also has fourteen patterns of conjugation. Go through the conjugations of (الفِعلُ المُضَارِعُ)in the below column. The conjugation of the past tense is also being repeated to give a proper understanding of both:

Letters prefixed to make المُضَارِعُ	Meaning	المُضَارِعُ	المَاضِي	الضَّمِيرُ
ي	He does	يَفْعَلُ	فَعَلَ	هُوَ
ي	They do	يَفْعَلاَن	فَعَلاَ	هُمَا
ي	They do	يَفْعَلُوْنَ	فَعَلُوْا	هُمْ
ت	She does	تَفْعَلُ	فَعَلَتْ	هِيَ
ت	They do	تَفْعَلاَن	فَعَلَتَا	هُمَا
ي	They do	يَفْعَلنَ	فَعَلنَ	هُنَّ
ت	You do	تَفْعَلُ	فَعَلتَ	أنْتَ
ت	You do	تَفْعَلاَن	فَعَلتُمَا	أنْتُمَا
ت	You do	تَفْعَلُوْنَ	فَعَلتُمْ	أنْتُمْ
ت	You do	تَفْعَلِيْنَ	فَعَلتِ	أنْتِ
ت	You do	تَفْعَلاَن	فَعَلتُمَا	أنْتُمَا
ت	You do	تَفْعَلنَ	فَعَلتُنَّ	أنْتُنَّ
أ	I do	أفْعَلُ	فَعَلتُ	أنَا
ن	We do	نَفْعَلُ	فَعَلنَا	نَحْنُ

If you compare both the past and present/future tenses you can observe the changes that took place in المُضَارِعُ in comparison to المَاضِي.

There are four letters (ي, ت, أ, ن)which are prefixed to (الفِعْلُ المَاضِي)to turn it into (الفِعْلُ المُضَارِعُ).

Besides those letters certain other changes also take place in the end of the past tense while turning it into the present/future tense which you can see in the column of conjugations of both the verbs. These are either "نِ" with kasra for (dual) or "نَ" with fat-ha for (plural) or some other changes in the vowel mark.

Usage of (الفِعْلُ المُضَارِعُ)is being given in the following column through sentences which will help you understand it well:

The teacher writes on the black board.	يَكْتُبُ المُعَلِّمُ عَلي السَّبُّوْرَةِ السَّوْدَاء
The students read the journals.	الطُّلاَّبُ يَقْرَأوُوْنَ الجَرَائِدَ
The two guards stand on the door.	الحَارِسَانِ يَقِفَانِ عَلي البَابِ
The labourers work in the factory.	العُمَّالُ يَعْمَلُوْنَ فِي المَصْنَع
The lady doctor checks up the patients	تُفحِّصُ الطَّبِيْبَةُ المَرْضَي
The two maids cook the food.	الخَادِمَتَانِ تَطْبَخَانِ الطَّعَامَ
The models present the winter clothes.	عَارِضَاتُ الأَزْيَاءِ يُقَدِّمْنَ المَلاَبِسَ الشَّتْوِيَة
Do you eat rice every day?	هَلْ تَأكُلُ الأَرُزَّ كُلَّ يَوْمٍ؟
Both of you work in the national bank.	تَعْمَلاَنِ فِيْ المَصْرَفِ الوَطَنِي
And he works in the President's office.	وَ هُوَ يَعْمَلُ فِي مَكْتَبِ الرَّئِيس
You always sleep early.	تَنَا مُوْنَ مُبَكِّراً دَائِماً
You sit in the front seat.	تَجْلِسِيْنَ فِي المَقْعَدِ الأَمَامِي
Why do you beat this young man?	لِمَاذَا تَضْرِبَانِ هَذَا الشَّابِّ؟

You buy summer clothes from Dubai.	تَشْتَرِيْنَ المَلَابِسَ الصَّيْفِيَّة مِنْ دُبَيْ
I play football.	اَلْعَبُ كُرَةَ القَدَم
We assemble in the field every morning.	نَجْتَمِعُ فِي المَيْدَان كُلَّ صَبَاح

In this column (المُضَارِعُ)has been used in different ways. All the cases of singular, dual and plural along with masculine and feminine have been used so you could learn how to use them effectively.

Structure of the sentence remains the same as it was in the past tense where a verb is brought first followed by a subject and in the end an object is brought like in the below example:

Subject +verb+ object	اَلفِعْلُ المُضَارِعُ+ الفَاعِلُ+المَفْعُوْلُ
The boys eat the food.	يَأكُلُ +الْأَوْلَادُ+الطَّعَامَ= يَأكُلُ الْأَوْلَادُ الطَّعَامَ

The object can also be brought as “preposition” (حَرْفُ الجَار)and (المَجْرُوْرُ)like in the example given as under:

The children sleep on the bed.	يَنَامُ +الْأَطْفَالُ+عَلَي السَّرِيْر=يَنَامُ الْأَطْفَالُ عَلَي السَّرِيْر

Use of "س" and "سَوْفَ"

Till now you have read the examples of (الفِعْلُ المُضَارِعُ)which give the meaning of present tense. However, if you prefix the letters "س" and "سَوْفَ" to (المُضَارِعُ)then meaning of it will be fixed exclusively for future tense. See the examples below:

My father shall go to Mecca.	سَيُسَافِرُ أَبِيْ اِلَي مَكَّة
The company will give you the prize.	سَوْفَ تُعْطِيْكَ الشَّرِكَةُ الجَائِزَة

Note: Remember it well that the letter "س" gives the meaning of near future whereas "سَوْفَ" gives the meaning of distant future.

Vocabulary:

The basket ball	كُرَةُ السلَةِ
To sleep	نَامَ \يَنَامُ\ نَوْمَةً
Early	مُبَكِّراً
Tomorrow	بُكْرَةً\ غداً
Today	اَليَوْمُ
Yesterday	أمْس
To write	كَتَبَ\ يَكْتُبُ\كِتَابَةً
The teacher	المُعَلِّمُ\المُعَلِّمُوْنَ
The black board	السُّبُّوْرَةُ السَّوْدَاءُ
To read	قرَأ\يَقرَأ\قِراءَةً
A student	طَالِبٌ\طُلاَبٌ
The journal	اَلجَرِيْدَةُ\ الجَرَائِدُ
The guard	اَلحَارِسُ\ اَلحَارِسُوْنَ
To stand	وَقَفَ\ يَقِفُ\وَقْفاً وَوُقُوْفاً
A door	بَابٌ\أبْوَابٌ
A labourer	عَامِلٌ\عُمَّالٌ
To check up	فحّصَ\ يُفَحِّصُ\تَفْحِيْصاً
The model	عَارِضَةُ الأزْيَاءِ
To present	قَدَّمَ\يُقَدِّمُ\تَقْدِيْماً
The winter clothes	المَلاَبِسُ الشَّتْوِيَّةُ
The summer clothes	اَلمَلاَبِسُ الصَّيْفِيَّةُ
The national bank	اَلمَصْرَفُ الوَطَنِي
The front seat	اَلمَقْعَدُ الأمَامِي
To purchase	اشْتَرَي\يَشْتَرِيْ\اِشْتِرَاءاً
Foot ball	كُرَةُ القَدَمِ
To assemble	اِجْتَمَعَ\يَجْتَمِعُ\اِجْتِمَاعاً
The field	اَلمَيْدَانُ\المَيَادِيْنُ

Exercise-1

Complete the conjugations of (المُضَارِعُ)for the below mentioned verbs and memorize them:

(1) يَلْعَبُ (he plays)
(2) يَفْتَحُ (he opens)
(3) يَعْمَلُ (he works)

Exercise-2

Translate into English:

(1) Akram takes tea.
(2) The shopkeeper sells wheat.
(3) Fatima will go to the College.
(4) Zaheer will play basket ball.
(5) You sleep early.

Hints: يَشْرَبُ (he drinks/takes sth) , صَاحِبُ الدُّكَّان (the shopkeeper) , يَبِيْعُ (he sells) , القَمْحُ (the wheat) , سَتَذْهَبُ (she will go) , الكُلِّيَّةُ (the College) ,يَلْعَبُ (he plays) .

Chapter 17
Negative of past tense

As you know about the past tense and its conjugations you should now know how to make a "negative verbal sentence with (الْمَاضِي)". The structure of the tense will remain the same.

You just have to prefix the word (مَا)to the past tense and it will turn into a negative verbal sentence. Have a look at the structure first and then some model sentences will be given to help you understand it well.

Structure of the sentence:

Subject + did not+ verb + object	مَا + الفِعْلُ المَاضِي+ الفَاعِلُ+المَفعُوْلُ
The guest did not eat the food.	مَا + أكَلَ + الضَّيْفُ + الطَّعَامَ

Just observe both sentences, Arabic as well as English, and their structure to know about it and practice it in your daily conversation.

In the below column some model sentences are being given so you can learn how to make a negative verbal sentence and use it without committing any mistake.

The guests did not eat the food.	مَا أكَلَ الضُيُوْفُ الطَّعَامَ
Hamid and Majid did not play yesterday.	حَامِدٌ وَ مَاجِدٌ مَا لعِبَا أمْس
The relatives did not sleep last night.	الْأقْرِبَاءُ مَا نَامُوْا الْبَارِحَة
My mother did not cook food today.	مَا طَبَخَتْ أُمِّيْ الطَّعَامَ الْيَوْمَ
Fatima and Khadija did not go to the college.	فاطِمَةُ وَ خَدِيْجَةُ مَا ذهَبَتَا إلي الكُلِّيَّةِ
The nurses did not turn up today.	المُمَرِّضَاتُ مَا حَضَرْنَ اليَوْمَ

Did you not hear the news?	أمَا سَمِعْتَ الْأَخْبَارَ؟
You (both) did not sit in the drawing room.	مَا جَلَسْتُمَا فِيْ غُرْفَةِ الإِسْتِقْبَال
You did not return from the market in time.	مَا رَجَعْتُمْ مِنَ السُّوْق فِي المِيْعَادِ
You did not come to visit my father.	مَا جِئْتِ لِزِيَارَةِ أَبِيْ
You (both) did not stay in the hotel.	مَا مَكَثْتُمَا فِي الْفُنْدُق
You did not listen to the songs.	مَا سَمِعْتُنَّ الْأَغَانِي
I did not open the door of the office.	مَا فَتَحْتُ بَابَ الْمَكْتَبِ
We never entered this city.	مَا دَخَلْنَا هَذِهِ الْمَدِيْنَة قَطُّ

Vocabulary:

Coffee	الْقَهْوَةُ
To play	لعِبَ\يَلْعَبُ\لعْبًا
The class room	الْفَصْلُ
Last night	الْبَارِحَةُ
Tonight	اللَّيْلَة
The player	اللَّاعِبُ\اللَّاعِبُوْنَ
To cook	طَبَخَ\يَطْبَخُ\طبْخًا
To train	دَرَّبَ\يُدَرِّبُ\تَدْرِيْباً
To go	ذَهَبَ\يَذْهَبُ\ذِهَاباً
The match	الْمُبَارَاةُ
The college	الْكُلِّيَّةُ
To send	أرْسَلَ\يُرْسِلُ\إرْسَالاً
The lady teacher	الْمُعَلِّمَةُ\ الْمُعَلِّمَاتُ

To appear/to turn up	حَضَرَ\يَحْضُرُ\حُضُوْراً
The gift	الْهَدِيَّةُ\ الْهَدَايَا
To listen	سَمِعَ\ يَسْمَعُ\سَمْعاً وَ سَمَاعَة
Cinema hall	دَارُ السَّيْنِمَا
News	خَبَرٌ\أَخْبَارٌ
To sit	جَلَسَ\يَجْلِسُ\جُلُوْساً
Ever	قَطُّ
Drawing room	غُرْفَةُ الْإِسْتِقْبَال
To enter	دَخَلَ\يَدْخُلُ\دُخُوْلاً
The door	الْبَابُ\الْأَبْوَابُ
On time	فِي الْمِيْعَادِ
To open	فَتَحَ\يَفْتَحُ\فَتْحاً
To visit	زَارَ\يَزُوْرُ\زِيَارَةً
Visit	زِيَارَةٌ
England	إِنْجِلْتَرَا
To stay	مَكَثَ\يَمْكُثُ\مُكُوْثاً
The song	الْأُغْنِيَةُ\ الْأَغَانِي
Together	مَعَاً
The train	الْقِطَارُ
To leave	تَرَكَ\يَتْرُكُ\تَرْكاً

Exercise-1

Make negative verbal sentence from the below given examples and translate them into English.

جَلسَ الطُّلاَبُ فِي الفَصْلِ
اللَّاعِبُوْنَ دَرَّبُوْا لِلمُبَارَاةِ
أرْسَلَتِ المُعَلَّمَاتُ الهَدَايَا إلي المُدِيرِ
النِّسَاءُ خَرَجْنَ مِنَ البَيْتِ
ذَهَبْتَ إلي دَارِ السِّيْنَمَا أمْس
مَكَثْتُ فِيْ إنْجَلتَرَا لِيَوْمَيْن
شَرِبْنَا القَهْوَةَ مَعَاً
نَزَلتُمْ مِنَ القِطَارِ اليَوْمَ

Exercise-2

Complete the conjugations of the following verbs and form at least five negative verbal sentences.

مَا شَرِبَ (He did not drink) .
مَانَصَرَ (He did not help) .
مَا قَتَلَ (He did not kill) .
مَا وَقَعَ (H e did not fall) .
مَا نَزَلَ (He did not come down) .

Chapter 18
Negative of present/ future tense

You have read that a negative verbal sentence of (الْمَاضِي)or past tense is made by prefixing the word (مَا)to it.
Likewise, you can make a negative verbal sentence of (الْمُضَارِعُ)or present/future tenses by prefixing (لَمْ)and (لَا)to it. Look at the below structure to understand it properly:

Subject+ did not+ verb+ object.	لَمْ + اَلفِعْلُ المُضَارِعُ + الفَاعِلُ+ المَفْعُوْلُ
The guest did not eat the food.	لَمْ يَأْكُلْ الضَّيْفُ الطَّعَامَ
Subject + does not+ verb+ object.	لَا + اَلفِعْلُ المُضَارِعُ+ الفَاعِلُ+ المَفْعُوْلُ
Nobody helps the poor. The Muslim does not drink the wine.	لَا يَنْصُرُ أَحَدٌ الضَّعِيْفَ لَا يَشْرَبُ المُسْلِمُ الخَمْرَ

You must be a bit confused after reading the first example of negative verbal sentence where the word (لَمْ)has been prefixed to (الْمُضَارِعُ)as it has turned the meaning of present/future tense into past tense. But you should never be confused about it as it acts like that only. Whenever the word (لَمْ)will be prefixed to (الْمُضَارِعُ)it will give the meaning of past tense only.
Not only that. The word (لَمْ)also brings another change in (الْمُضَارِعُ). It applies vowel mark "sukun" on the last letter of the said verb as it appears in the above example.
لَمْ also drops the letters و,ا, and ي, from a present/future tense whose middle or last letter happens to be having any of these. So present tense (يَقُوْلُ)becomes (لَمْ يَقُلْ)after dropping the middle letter (و)from it and (يَدْعُوْ)becomes (لَمْ يَدْعُ). The same way (يَرْمِي)becomes (لَمْ يَرْمِ) after dropping the letter (ي)from the end of the verb.

However, when the word (لا)will be prefixed to (المُضَارِعُ)it will give the meaning of present and future tenses as it is evident from the example above.

Now read some model sentences and observe them carefully to grasp how it works:

No one entered the room.	لَمْ يَدْخُلْ أحَدٌ فِي الغُرْفَةِ
The CEO did not travel to New York.	لَمْ يُسَافِرْ الرَّئِيسُ التَّنفِيْذِيْ إلي نِيُويَوْرْك
Hamida did not sit with me.	لَمْ تَجْلِسْ حَمِيْدَةُ مَعِي
The student does not read the book.	لا يقرأ الطَّالِبُ الكِتَاب
The government does not demand tax from the poor.	لاتَطلبُ الحُكُوْمَةُ الضَّرِيْبَةَ مِنَ الفُقَرَاء
The buses don't run on the holiday.	لا تَسِيْرُ البَاصَاتُ يَوْمَ العُطْلَةِ
The media does not publish the news of corruption.	لا يَطْبَعُ الإعْلامُ أخْبَارَالفَسَادِ
The workers do not get their wages.	لا يَجِدُ العُمَّالُ أجُوْرَهُمْ
The court did not give justice to the women.	لَمْ تُقَدِّمْ المَحْكَمَةُ العَدْلَ إلِيْ النِّسَاءِ
The criminals don't fear of the Police.	لا يَخَافُ المُجْرِمُوْنَ مِنَ الشُّرْطَةِ
The children do not respect their parents.	لا يُكْرِمُ الأَوْلادُ أبَوَيْهِمْ

Use of particle of negation (لَنْ)

Like the particle of negative (لا)there is another particle of negative called (لَنْ)which is prefixed to (الفِعْلُ المُضَارِعُ)and fixes its meaning exclusively for future tense. Look at some of the examples below:

Meaning	لنْ + المُضارِعُ + الفَاعِلُ + المَفْعُوْلُ
My son will never fail in the exam.	لنْ يَفْشَلَ إِبْنِيْ فِي الِامْتِحَانِ
You will never ever push out the strangers.	لنْ تَطْرُدَ الغُرَبَاءَ أبَداً
The workers will never work in the factories.	لنْ يَعْمَلَ العُمَّالُ في المَصَانِعِ
I will never give you money to buy the wine.	لنْ أعْطِيَكَ النُّقُوْدَ لِشِراءِ الخَمْرِ
The director will never allow you to enter.	لنْ يَسْمَحَ لكَ المُدِيْرُ بِالدُّخُوْلِ
The children will never sleep before the dinner.	لنْ يَنَامَ الأطفَالُ قبْلَ العَشَاءِ

The particle of negation (لنْ)always gives vowel mark "Fat-ha" to the last letter of (الفِعْلُ المُضَارِعُ)as you can see in the above examples.
So you can see that the structure of the sentence will be as below:

The students will never enter the class.	لنْ + يَدْخُلَ+ الطُّلاَّبُ + فِي الفَصْلِ

Vocabulary:

To fail	فشِلَ\يَفشَلُ\فشْلاً
The exam	الِامْتِحَانُ
To push out	طرَدَ\يَطْرُدُ\طرْداً
The stranger	الغرِيْبُ\الغُرَبَاءُ
To give	أعْطي\يُعْطِي\إعْطاءا
Money	النَّقْدُ\ النُّقُوْدُ

To buy	شِرَاءٌ
Wine	اَلْخَمْرُ\ اَلْخُمُوْرُ
To allow	سَمَحَ\يَسْمَحُ\سَمْحاً وَ سَمَاحَةٌ
Entry	اَلدُّخُوْلُ
The dinner	اَلعَشَاءُ
The lunch	اَلغَدَاءُ
To throw	رَمَي\يَرْمِي\رَمْيًا
To wrap up	طوَي\يَطْوِي\طوِيً
To invite	دَعَا\يَدْعُوْ\دَعْوَةً
To walk	مَشَي\يَمْشِي\مَشْيًا
The weak	اَلضَّعِيْفُ\ اَلضُّعَفَاءُ
To pay/to push	دَفَعَ\ يَدْفَعُ\دَفْعاً
The company	اَلشَّرِكَةُ\ اَلشَّرِكَاتُ
Salary	رَاتِبٌ\ رَوَاتِبُ
To listen to	اِسْتَمَعَ\ يَسْتَمِعُ\اِسْتِمَاعاً
Advice	نَصِيْحَةٌ\ نَصَائِحُ
The parents	اَلأَبَوَيْن
To carry	حَمَلَ\ يَحْمِلُ\ حَمْلاً
The card	اَلبطَاقَةُ
To arrest	قَبَضَ\يَقْبِضُ\قَبْضاً عَلَيْ
The police	اَلشُّرْطَةُ
Thief	لِصٌّ\لُصُوْصٌ
To come	أَتَي\يَأْتِي\إِتْيَانًا
Bird	طَيْرٌ\طُيُوْرٌ
This year	هَذِهِ السَّنَة
The protester	اَلمُتَظَاهِرُ\ اَلمُتَظَاهِرُوْنَ
Chamber of the President	غُرْفَةُ الرَّئِيْس

Exercise-1

Translate the following into English:

لا يَمْشِيْ الرَّجُلُ الضَّعِيْفُ سَرِيْعاً
لا تَدْفَعُ الشَّرِكَةُ الرَّوَاتِبَ إلِي العُمَّال
لا يَسْتَمِعُ الْأَوْلادُ إلِيْ نَصَائح أَبَوَيْهِمْ
لَنْ تَقْبضَ الشُّرْطَةُ عَلي اللُّصُوْص

Exercise-2

Complete the sentences by using the particles of negative (لَمْ)and (لا)
.

......يَرْجِع أبِي أَمْس
الحَقُّ......يَمُوْتُ
......يَنْجَحْ أحَدٌ في الِامْتِحَان
المُعَلِّمُوْنَ......يَضْرِبُوْنَ الطُّلَّابَ
الدَّنِئُ........يُكْرِمُ أحَداً

Chapter 19
The subject

A doer is called (الفَاعِلُ)in Arabic. For convenience it has been termed as "subject" in this book. You should differentiate between "subject with predicate" and "subject as doer" while going through different examples avoiding confusion.

In a verbal sentence the subject (الفَاعِلُ)either will be visible or hidden. A few examples of both visible and hidden cases are being provided in the below column. Read them carefully to know it well:

Hidden subject is:	Verbal sentence	Visible subject is:	Verbal sentence
ضرَبْتَ in (ت) أنتَ	ضَرَبْتَ الطِّفْلَ	اَلوَلَدُ	يَلعَبُ الوَلَدُ فِي المَيْدَان
سَرَقُوْا in (وا) هُمْ	سَرَقُوْا الكِتَابَ	البِنْتُ	تَدْرُسُ البِنْتُ الكِتَابَ
دَفعْتُ in (تُ) أنَا	دَفعْتُ الثَّمَنَ	اَلسَّائِقَان	يَنَامُ السَّائِقَان
نَأكُلُ in نَحْنُ (ن)	نَأكُلُ المَوْزَ	اَلرِّجَالُ	يَعْمَلُ الرِّجَالُ

Object

Unlike subject (الفَاعِلُ)the object (المَفْعُوْلُ)always remains visible. However, it can either be a noun or a pronoun or even a combination of preposition+ noun (حَرْفُ الجَارِوَ المَجْرُوْرُ).

Some examples are being given to further illustrate the point:

Description	Verbal sentence
Here the object is a noun (الطَّعَامَ)	أكَلَ الضُّيُوْفُ الطَّعَامَ
The object is prep+ noun (فِيْ الفَصْلِ)	دَخَلَ الطُّلاَّبُ فِي الفَصْلِ
The object is personal pronoun (كَ)	مَنْ ضَرَبَكَ؟

You have already read in the previous chapters that a sentence starting with a verb is called verbal sentence or (الجُمْلَةُ الفِعْلِيَّةُ)and its structure is as below:

Subject + verb + object.	الفِعْلُ + الفَاعِلُ + المَفعُولُ
The teacher read the journals.	قرأ المُدَرِّسُ الجَرَائِدَ
The rich people live in the flat.	يَسْكُنُ الْأَغْنِيَاءُ فِي الشُّقَّةِ

You also know that vowel mark of the subject (الفَاعِلُ)is "Damma" and vowel mark of the object (المَفعُولُ)is "Fat-ha" as you have already seen in several examples.

Vocabulary:

Doctor	طبِيبٌ\أطِبَّاءُ
Europe	أوْرُبَّا
To repair	رَمَّمَ\يُرَمِّمُ\تَرْمِيماً
The mechanic	المَيْكَانِيْكِيْ
To send	أنْزَلَ\يُنْزِلُ\إنْزالا
The rain	المَطرُ\ الأمْطارُ
To kneed	عَجَنَ\يَعْجِنُ\عَجْناً وَعَجِيْناً
The dough	الطَّحِيْنُ
To smoke	دَخَّنَ\يُدَخِّنُ\تَدْخِيْناً
The cigarette	السِّيْجَارَةُ
To live	سَكَنَ\يَسْكُنُ\سَكَناً
Rich	غَنِيٌّ\ أغْنِيَاءُ
The flat	الشَّقَّةُ\ الشَّقَّاتُ

Exercise-1

Find out subjects and objects in the following sentences:

يَذْهَبُ الأَطِبَّاءُ إِلي أورُبَّا

يرَمِّمُ المِيْكَانِيْكِيُّونَ السَيَّارَةَ

يُنْزِلُ اللهُ الأَمْطَارَ

تَعْجِنُ الأُمُّ الطَّحِيْنَ

يُدَخِّنُ الطُّلاَّبُ السِّيْجَارَةَ

Exercise-2

Fill in the blanks with appropriate subjects and objects:

مَدَّ......... رِجْلَهُ

يَدْخُلُ الأَطْفَالُ.........كُلَّ يَوْمٍ

عَمِيْدُ الكُلِّيَّةِ أَعْطَاهُ ....

Hints: اَلمَرِيْضُ (the patient) , فِي الحَدِيْقَةِ (in the park) , اَلجَائِزَةَ (The prize) .

Chapter 20
Imperative Verb

If you happen to be sitting in a restaurant how will you place your order? Which verb will you use when you reach home and find the door of your house bolted from inside? That's where you have to use imperative verb. This imperative verb is called (فِعْلُ الْأَمْر)in Arabic. This verb is used for placing order, making a request and giving advice.

Imperative verb is made from present/future tense (الفِعْلُ المُضَارِعُ)and has only six following patterns of conjugation instead of fourteen as was the case in the past and present tenses. These patterns are as under:

Only six patterns of conjugations	فِعْلُ الْأَمْر	المُضَارِعُ	الضَّمَائِرُ
	X	يَفْعَلُ	هُوَ
	X	يَفْعَلَانِ	هُمَا
	X	يَفْعَلُوْنَ	هُمْ
	X	تَفْعَلُ	هِيَ
	X	تَفْعَلَانِ	هُمَا
	X	يَفْعَلْنَ	هُنَّ
Masculine singular (you do) (MS)	إِفْعَلْ	تَفْعَلُ	أَنْتَ
Masculine dual (you do) (MD)	إِفْعَلَا	تَفْعَلَانِ	أَنْتُمَا
Masculine plural (you do) (MP)	إِفْعَلُوْا	تَفْعَلُوْنَ	أَنْتُمْ
Feminine singular (you do) (FS)	إِفْعَلِيْ	تَفْعَلِيْنَ	أَنْتِ
Feminine dual (you do) (FD)	إِفْعَلَا	تَفْعَلَانِ	أَنْتُمَا
Feminine plural (you do) (FP)	إِفْعَلْنَ	تَفْعَلْنَ	أَنْتُنَّ
	X	أَفْعَلُ	أَنَا
	X	نَفْعَلُ	نَحْنُ

Things to remember:

(فِعْلُ الْأَمْر) Imperative verb is made from (الْفِعْلُ الْمُضَارِعُ)present/future tense.

Last letter of (فِعْلُ الْأَمْر)always remains vowel-less except when it is followed by a definite noun. In that case sukun is replaced with vowel mark "kasra". Example:

Open the door. Respect the guest.	إفْتَحِ البَابَ أكْرِمِ الضَّيْفَ

There are certain rules for making (فِعْلُ الْأَمْر)or imperative verb from (الْفِعْلُ الْمُضَارِعُ). These are as below:

(a) if the second letter of (الْفِعْلُ الْمُضَارِعُ)is having sukun then alif اَلْأَلِفُ (ا)will be prefixed while making (فِعْلُ الْأَمْر)and this alif (ا)will get vowel mark "Dam-ma" if the second last letter of (الْفِعْلُ الْمُضَارِعُ) carries vowel mark "Damma". **Example:**

Meaning	فِعْلُ الْأَمْر	الْفِعْلُ الْمُضَارِعُ
Help.	أُنْصُرْ	يَنْصُرُ
Write.	أُكْتُبْ	يَكْتُبُ

(b) If the second last letter of (الْفِعْلُ الْمُضَارِعُ)carries vowel mark "kas-ra" or "Fat-ha" then in both such cases the prefixed alif (ا)will carry only "kas-ra". **Example:**

Meanings	فِعْلُ الْأَمْر	الْفِعْلُ الْمُضَارِعُ
Beat.	إضْرِبْ	يَضْرِبُ
Open.	إفْتَحْ	يَفْتَحُ

(c) However, if the second letter of (الْفِعْلُ الْمُضَارِعُ)is carrying vowel mark "Damma" or "Fat-ha" then the imperative verb (فِعْلُ الْأَمْر)will be made by dropping the first letter of (الْمُضَارِعُ)and also dropping any of the letters like (و,ا,ي)from the second last letter of (المُضَارِعُ). **Example:**

Meaning	فِعْلُ الْأمْر	الفِعْلُ المُضَارِعُ
Say.	قُلْ	يَقُوْلُ
Stand up.	قُمْ	يَقُوْمُ
Leave.	دَعْ	يَدَعُ

Nouns used as (فِعْلُ الْأمْر)in Arabic:

There are two nouns in Arabic which are always used as imperative verbs. These are:

هَاتِ (Bring) .

تَعَالَ (Come) .

These two nouns also have six patterns of conjugation just like any normal imperative verb (فِعْلُ الْأمْر). The conjugations are given in the column as under:

Come	تَعَالَ تَعَالَيَا تَعَالَوْا تَعَالِيْ تَعَالَيَا تَعَالَيْنَ	Bring	هَاتِ هَاتِيَا هَاتُوْا هَاتِيْ هَاتِيَا هَاتِيْنَ

Chapter 21
Negative imperative verb

Like imperative verb (فِعْلُ الْأَمْرِ)the negative imperative verb (فِعْلُ النَّهْيِ) also has six patterns of conjugations. Negative imperative verb is also made from (الفِعْلُ المُضَارِعُ)just like (فِعْلُ الْأَمْرِ). To make a negative imperative verb you have to prefix the particle of negation (لَا)to (المُضَارِعُ)and the six patterns of conjugation will be as below:

Meaning	فِعْلُ النَّهْيِ	Meaning	فِعْلُ النَّهْيِ
Do not beat.	لَا تَضْرِبِيْ لَا تَضْرِبَا لَا تَضْرِبْنَ	Do not beat.	لَا تَضْرِبْ لَا تَضْرِبَا لَا تَضْرِبُوْا

The structure of the sentence for both the imperative and negative imperative verbs will be as below:

Open the door.	إِفْتَحْ + البَابَ	فِعْلُ الْأَمْرِ
Do not beat the weak.	لَا + تَضْرِبِ + الضَّعِيْفَ	فِعْلُ النَّهْيِ

As you can see there is no visible subject (الفَاعِلُ)in any of the above two model sentences for imperative and negative imperative sentences. The subject always remains hidden in such sentences.
Some times even the object (المَفْعُوْلُ)is not required as only imperative and negative imperative verbs alone complete the sentences like in:

Do not move. Do not sit. Do not talk.	لَاتَتَحَرَّكْ لَا تَجْلِسْ لَا تَتَحَدَّثْ	Go. Stop. Stand up.	إِذْهَبْ قِفْ قُمْ

Exercise-1

Make imperative and negative imperative verbs from the below given (الفِعْلُ المُضَارِعُ)and write their patterns of conjugations:

1. يَتْعَبُ (he gets tired) .
2. يَجْلِسُ (he sits) .
3. يَأكُلُ (he eats) .
4. يَزُوْرُ (he visits) .

Exercise-2

Translate into Arabic:

1. Do not eat sweets.
2. Do not sit on the road.
3. Sleep in your room.
4. Read newspaper on time.
5. Do not go outside the house.

Hints: الحَلاوَي (the sweets) , نَامَ/يَنَامُ (to sleep) , الجَرَائدُ (the journals) , الصَّحِيْفَة (the newspaper) , فِيْ المِيْعَادِ (on time) , خَارِجَ (outside) .

Chapter 22
Passive voice

You have read about the Active Voice (الفِعْلُ المَعْرُوفُ)in the previous chapters and observed the examples and model sentences related to it.

As you are aware that a verbal sentence with an Active voice is made up of three components i.e. verb, subject and object. However, in a verbal sentence with a passive voice the sentence is formed without a subject as it is replaced by the object (المَفْعُوْلُ)and this object is called "replacement of subject" or (نَائِبُ الفَاعِل). But first look at the conjugation of Passive voice in the below column so you can have proper idea about it. Here is the past tense of Active voice (الفِعْلُ المَعْرُوْفُ)along with the conjugations of the passive voice (الفِعْلُ المَجْهُوْلُ) :

Meaning	الفِعْلُ المَجْهُوْلُ	الفِعْلُ المَعْرُوْفُ	الضَّمَائِرُ
He was beaten. They were beaten. They were beaten.	ضُرِبَ ضُرِبَا ضُرِبُوْا	ضَرَبَ ضَرَبَا ضَرَبُوْا	هُوَ هُمَا هُمْ
She was beaten. They were beaten. They were beaten.	ضُرِبَتْ ضُرِبَتَا ضُرِبْنَ	ضَرَبَتْ ضَرَبَتَا ضَرَبْنَ	هِيَ هُمَا هُنَّ
You were beaten. You were beaten. You were beaten.	ضُرِبْتَ ضُرِبْتُمَا ضُرِبْتُمْ	ضَرَبْتَ ضَرَبْتُمَا ضَرَبْتُمْ	أنْتَ أنْتُمَا أنْتُمْ
You were beaten. You were beaten. You were beaten.	ضُرِبْتِ ضُرِبْتُمَا ضُرِبْتُنَّ	ضَرَبْتِ ضَرَبْتُمَا ضَرَبْتُنَّ	أنْتِ أنْتُمَا أنْتُنَّ
I was beaten. We were beaten.	ضُرِبْتُ ضُرِبْنَا	ضَرَبْتُ ضَرَبْنَا	أنَا نَحْنُ

Now have a look at the below structure of the sentences. This will help you understand passive voice properly:

Meaning (passive)	اَلفِعْلُ + نَائِبُ الفَاعِلِ	**Meaning (Active)**	الفِعْلُ+ الفَاعِلُ+المَفْعُولُ
The letter was written.	كُتِبَتِ الرِّسَالَةُ	Hamid wrote the letter.	كَتَبَ حَامِدٌ الرِّسَالَة
The thief was beaten.	ضُرِبَ اللِّصُّ	Adil beat the thief.	ضَرَبَ عَادِلٌ اللِّصَّ

So you can observe the difference in active voice (الفِعْلُ المَعْرُوْفُ)and passive voice (الفِعْلُ المَجْهُوْلُ).
In the Arbaic sentences of Active voice the structure is like this:
(Verb + subject + object)
Whereas the structure of the Arbic sentence of the passive voice is as under:
(Verb + replacement of the subject)
Some more model sentences are here which may provide you with more clarity. Just go through them and read out loudly:

Passive voice.	الفِعْلُ المَجْهُوْلُ
The door was knocked and the visitor was taken in.	دُقَّ البَابُ وُ أُدْخِلَ الزَّائِرُ
The house was destroyed and the bridge was built.	هُدِّمَ البَيْتُ وُ بُنِيَ الجِسْرُ
The criminal was asked to appear before the judge.	طُلِبَ المُجْرِمُ لِلحُضُوْرِأَمَامَ القَاضِي
The thief was tied with the rope.	شُدَّ السَّارِقُ بِا لحَبْلِ
The house was painted with the colors.	طُلِيَ البَيْتُ بِالألوَان
The engineer was sent to the ministry.	أُرْسِلَ المُهَنْدِسُ إلِي الوَزَارَةِ

The help was provided to the needy people. The criminals were forgiven.	قُدِّمَتِ المَعُوْنَةُ إِلَيْ المُحتَاجِيْنَ عُفِيَ عَنِ المُجْرِمِيْنَ

Passive voice of (المُضَارِعُ)

Like the past tense (الفِعْلُ المَاضِي)the present\future tense (المُضَارِعُ)also has its own passive voice. The conjugation of the passive voice of (المُضَارِع)is as below:

Description.	الفِعْلُ المَجْهُولُ	الفِعْلُ المَعْرُوْفُ	الضَّمَائِرُ
To make passive voice (الفِعْلُ المَجْهُوْلُ)the first letter of Active voice of (المُضَارِع)is given vowel mark "Damma" and the second last letter is given "Fat-ha" like in: يُكْتَبُ ,يُسْرَقُ ,يُفتَحُ ,يُكْذَبُ.	يُفْعَلُ يُفْعَلَانِ يُفْعَلُوْنَ	يَفْعَلُ يَفْعَلَانِ يَفْعَلُوْنَ	هُوَ هُمَا هُمْ
	تُفْعَلُ تُفْعَلَانِ يُفْعَلْنَ	تَفْعَلُ تَفْعَلَانِ يَفْعَلْنَ	هِيَ هُمَا هُنَّ
	تُفْعَلُ تُفْعَلَانِ تُفْعَلُوْنَ	تَفْعَلُ تَفْعَلَانِ تَفْعَلُوْنَ	أَنْتَ أَنْتُمَا أَنْتُمْ
	تُفْعَلِيْنَ تُفْعَلَانِ تُفْعَلْنَ	تَفْعَلِيْنَ تَفْعَلَانِ تَفْعَلْنَ	أَنْتِ أَنْتُمَا أَنْتُنَّ
	أُفْعَلُ نُفْعَلُ	أَفْعَلُ نَفْعَلُ	أَنَا نَحْنُ

Some model sentences about passive voice of (المُضَارِعُ):

	الفِعْلُ + نَائِبُ الفَاعِلِ
The taxes are taken from the rich.	تُؤْخَذُ الضَّرَائِبُ مِنَ الْأَغْنِيَاءِ
The film festival is held every year.	يُعْقَدُ الحَفْلُ السِّيْنَمَائِيْ كُلَّ سَنَةٍ
The wages are distributed among the workers.	تُقَسَّمُ الْأُجُوْرُ بَيْنَ العُمَّالِ

The sweets are distributed on the occasion of national festival.	تُوَزَّعُ الحَلَاوَيْ بِمُنَاسَبَةِ العِيْدِ الوَطَنِيْ
The student is beaten.	يُضْرَبُ الطَّالِبُ

Things to remember:

- Passive voice is called (الفِعْلُ المَجْهُوْلُ)in Arabic.
- Passive voice is made from intransitive verbs only.
- Active voice usually requires a subject and an object to complete the sentence, however in a Passive voice the object replaces the subject and is called “replacement of subject” or (نَائِبُ الفَاعِل).
- Passive voice of (الفِعْلُ المَاضِيْ)is made by giving vowel mark “Damma” to the first letter of (الفِعْلُ المَاضِيْ)and “Kas-ra” to the second last letter of the same as in: سُرِق,قُتِلَ,سُمِعَ,ضُرِبَ
- As far as (الفِعْلُ المُضَارِعُ)is concerned, the first letter of it is given vowel mark “Dam-ma” and the second last letter is given vowel mark “Fat-ha” as in: يُعْلَنُ,يُكْتَبُ

Chapter 23
Verbal Noun (To+verb/verb+ing)

Verbal noun or (المَصْدَرُ)is very important because you have to know it for various reasons and purposes while reading or writing or even speaking Arabic. You will also be required to know this noun while looking upto the dictionary. So how will you recognize a verbal noun? There is no specific rule or pattern of making it and only thorough reading and constant practice can help in this regard. However, you can at least know what it means and how to tackle it. You can learn this by reading the below examples. You should not forget that verbal nouns are made from verbs.

To make it simple let us see how it is used in English. The above structure i.e. (to+ first form of the verb) or (verb+ing) can help you.

"To go" or "going" in English have their equivalents in Arabic and they are called (المَصْدَرُ). In the below column you will find a list of verbs along with their verbal nouns which will help you understand it properly. Just go through this column of verbs and verbal nouns:

The verbal noun (to+verb)	المَاضِيْ \ المُضَارِعُ \ المَصْدَرُ
To go	ذَهَبَ \ يَذْهَبُ \ ذَهَاباً
To hear/to listen to	سَمِعَ \ يَسْمَعُ \سَمْعاً وسَمَاعَة
To eat	أكَلَ \ يَأكُلُ \ أكْلاً
To go past/ to pass	مَرَّ \ يَمُرُّ \ مَرّاً وَ مُرُوْراً
To stand	قَامَ \ يَقُوْمُ \ قِيَاماً
To visit	زَارَ \ يَزُوْرُ \ زِيَارَةً
To sleep	نَامَ \ يَنَامُ \ نَوْمَة وَنِيَاماً
To sit	جَلَسَ \ يَجْلِسُ \ جِلسَة وَ جُلُوْساً
To enter	دَخَلَ \ يَدْخُلُ \ دُخُوْلاً

You should read the Arabic part of the column in the order indicated right at the beginning of it. It means that first you will find past tense (الفِعْلُ المَاضِيْ)then present/future tense (المُضَارِعُ)and in the end you will find verbal noun (المَصْدَرُ).

Note:

You can use the verbal noun (المَصْدَرُ)as both definite and indefinite nouns. You can also use it as subject, noun qualified and adjective as per the need.

Chapter 24
Some important uses (Has/have+third form of the verb) (HAS/HAVE GONE)

If you come across any such expression in Arabic how will you say it? The below simplified way of forming sentences might help you if you keep the pattern in mind.

The structure of the sentence will be as below:

Subject + has/have + vbIII + object.	قَدْ + اَلفِعْلُ المَاضِيْ + الفَاعِلُ + المَفعُوْلُ
The guest has eaten the food.	قَدْ أَكَلَ الضَّيْفُ الطَّعَامَ
My father has gone to New York.	قَدْ ذَهَبَ أَبِيْ إِلَي نِيُوْ يَوْرَك
My sister has received the prize.	قَدْ نَالَتْ أُخْتِيْ الجَائِزَةَ

So, you can understand from the above examples and structure of the sentence that you can form a sentence on the above pattern for an expression mentioned at the beginning of this chapter.

In the above examples the particle (قَدْ)has been prefixed to the past tense (الفِعْلُ المَاضِيْ)to give the meaning of (has/have) . However, if the same particle (قَدْ)is prefixed to a present/future tense (الفِعْلُ المُضَارِعُ)it will give the meaning of "May". See the below examples:

	قَدْ + الفِعْلُ المُضَارِعُ + الفَاعِلُ+ المَفعُوْلُ
The minister may come to the village.	قَدْ يَأْتِيْ الوَزِيْرُ إِلَي القَرْيَةِ
It may rain today.	قَدْ يَنْزِلُ المَطرُ اليَوْمَ
The Prince may deliver the speech.	قَدْ يُلقِيْ الأَمِيْرُ الخِطَابَ

For expressions like:

1. The guest had eaten the food.
2. The dancers had performed their art.
3. The children had slept.

You should use the following structure of sentence in your every day conversation:

Subject+had+verbiii+object.	كَانَ+الفَاعِلُ+الفِعْلُ المَاضِيْ+المَفْعُوْلُ
The guest had eaten the food. The dancers had performed their art. The children had slept.	كَانَ الضَّيْفُ قَدْ أكَلَ الطَّعَامَ كَانَتِ الرَّاقِصَاتُ قَدْ قَدَّمْنَ فُنُونَهُنَّ كَانَ الأَطْفَالُ قَدْ نَامُوْا

(Has + to /have to + first form of the verb)
(He has to/ they have to study)
For such pattern of expression in Arabic you will be following the below given structure:

	يَضْطَرُّ+الفَاعِلُ+إِلىْ+المَجْرُوْر
The traders have to pay the tax. Ahmad has to study. The director has to scold.	يَضْطَرُّ التُّجَّارُ إلي دَفْعِ الضَّرِيْبَةِ يَضْطَرُّ أحْمَدُ إلي الدِّرَاسَةِ يَضْطَرُّ المُدِيْرُ إلي العِتَابِ

You saw in the above examples that the present/future tense or (المُضَارِعُ)of a verb (يَضْطَرُّ)has been used for the expression of (has to/have to) . However, the past tense (الفِعْلُ المَاضِيْ)of the same verb i.e (إِضْطَرَّ)is used for the below expression:
(The teacher had to beat the students)
Look at the structure of the sentence in the below column:

The teacher had to beat the student.	اِضْطَرَّ المُعَلِّمُ إلِيْ ضَرْبِ الطَّالِبِ

The lady doctor had to return.	إضْطَرَّتِ الطَّبِيْبَةُ إلي الرُّجُوْع
The President had to resign.	إضْطَرَّ الرَّئِيْسُ إلي الإسْتِقالةِ

Note: (اِضْطَرَّ\ يَضْطَرُّإلي)

The conjugations of present/futute tense (المُضَارِعْ)of the above verb is used for (has to/have to) and for (had to) the conjugations of the past tense (الفِعْلُ المَاضِي)of the same verb is used.
(Subject + has/had + noun)
(He has a mobile)
If you ever come across any such structure of the sentence in Arabic you should follow the below given easy and simple way:

Subject + has/have + noun.	عِنْدَ + الإسْمُ\ الضميرُ + الإسْمُ الثَّانِي
My brother has a new car.	عِنْدَ أخِيْ سَيَّارَةٌ جَدِيْدَةٌ
What do you have?	مَا هُوَ عِنْدَكَ؟
I have an expensive pen.	عِنْدِيْ قلمٌ ثَمِيْنٌ
Does your father also have a pen?	هَلْ عِنْدَ أبِيْكَ قلمٌ أيْضاً؟
No, he has a computer.	لا , عِنْدَهُ حَاسُوْبٌ آلِيٌّ
The principal has an important book.	عِنْدَ العَمِيْدِ كِتَابٌ مُهِمٌّ
And the director has an expensive mobile.	وَ عِنْدَ المُدِيْرِ جَوَّالٌ غَالٍ

However, for the expressions like "He had a new car" or "He had a book" the structure will remain the same but (كَانَ)and its other conjugations will be added. Have a look at the below structure of the sentence to understand it:

My brother had a new car.	كَانَتْ عِنْدَ أخِيْ سَيَّارَةٌ جَدِيْدَةٌ
What did you have?	مَاذَا كَانَ عِنْدَكَ؟

I had an expensive pen.	كَانَ عِنْدِيْ قلمٌ ثَمِيْنٌ
Did your father also have a pen?	هَلْ كَانَ عِنْدَ أبيْكَ قلمٌ أيْضاً؟
No, he had a computer.	لا ,كَانَ عِنْدَهُ حَاسُوْبٌ آلِيٌ
The principal had an important book.	كَانَ عِنْدَ العَمِيْدِ كِتَابٌ مُهمٌّ
And the director had an expensive mobile.	وَكَانَ عِنْدَ المُدِيْرِ جَوَّالٌ غَالٍ

Chapter 25
Relative pronouns (Who/which)

The relative pronouns or (الْأسمَاءُ المَوْصُوْلَةُ)are as below. Familiarize yourself first with these before going through the sentences based on their usage.

Relative pronouns	الْأسمَاءُ المَوْصُوْلَةُ	Relative pronouns	الْأسمَاءُ المَوْصُوْلَةُ
Who/ which (FS)	الّتِيْ	Who/ which (MS)	الّذِيْ
Who/ which (FD)	اللّتَان \ اللّتَيْن	Who/ which (MD)	الّذَان \ الّذَيْن
Who/ which (FP)	اللّاتِيْ \ اللّوَاتِي	Who/ which (MP)	الّذِيْنَ

So, you can now understand what are the relative pronouns or (الْأسمَاءُ المَوْصُوْلَةُ).

Dual of both the masculine and feminine relative pronouns has changed slightly as you can see. But if you could recall the chapter on "Dual" in this book you can easily understand that (الْألِفُ)is replaced with (اليَاءُ)in accusative and genitive cases.

Here are the model sentences in which relative pronouns have been used. Just read them slowly so you can learn how to use them as and when you need them:

Who is the person who eats banana?	مَنْ هُوَ الشَّخْصُ الّذِيْ يَأكُلُ المَوْزَ؟
He is my friend.	هُوَ صَدِيْقِيْ,
Is the student who got down the car your sister?	هَل الطَّالِبَةُ الّتِيْ نَزَلَتْ مِنَ السَّيَّارَةِ أخْتُكَ؟
No, the teacher who came out of the class is my sister.	لاَ, المُعَلِّمَةُ الّتِي خَرَجَتْ مِنَ الفَصْلِ أخْتِيْ

Who is the boy who plays in the playground?	مَنْ هُوَ الوَلَدُ الَّذِيْ يَلعَبُ فِيْ المَلعَبِ؟
The boy who plays in the playground is my son.	الوَلَدُ الَّذِيْ يَلعَبُ فِيْ المَلعَبِ إِبْنِيْ
And the two drivers who came out of the house are friends.	وَ السَّائِقَانِ اللَّذَانِ خَرَجَا مِنَ البَيْتِ صَدِيْقَانِ
And the two lady doctors who talk with each other are my friends' sisters.	وَ الطَّبِيْبَتَانِ اللَّتَانِ تَتَحَدَّثَتَانِ مَعًا أُخْتَاصَدِيْقِيْ
Who are these white men who greeted you?	مَنْ هَؤُلَاءِ الرِّجَالُ البِيْضُ اللَّذِيْنَ سَلَّمُوْا عَلَيْكَ؟
They are guests from Ireland.	هُمُ الضُّيُوْفُ مِنْ آيَرْلَنْدَا
And the businessmen who came down the train are from Africa.	وَ رِجَالُ الأَعْمَالِ اللَّذِيْنَ نَزَلُوْا مِنَ القِطَارِ مِنْ إِفْرِيْقِيَّا
The lady teachers who got late for the class are my sisters.	المُعَلِّمَاتُ اللَّوَاتِيْ تَأَخَّرْنَ لِلفَصْلِ أَخَوَاتِيْ

So, the structure of the sentence will be like this:

(المُضَافُ + المُضَافُ إِلَيْهِ = الخَبَرُ)	(الإِسْمُ + الإِسْمُ المَوْصُوْلُ+ الفِعْلُ+ الجَارُ وَ المَجْرُوْرُ= المُبْتَدَأُ)
إِبْنَتِيْ	الطَّالِبَةُ الَّتِيْ جَلَسَتْ عَلي الكُرْسِيِّ

It seems a bit complicated but if you try to read the above sentences patiently you will be able to understand that the sentence is based on the same structure as it was followed in the chapter on "subject and predicate".

You can also know the fact that a relative pronoun is brought as per the number and gender of the noun coming before it.

If a noun is singular masculine then the relative pronoun will also be brought as singular masculine. The same rule will apply to dual and plural cases.

A verb is brought right after the relative pronoun to elaborate the noun. This verb also has to be compatible with the number and gender of the noun coming before the relative pronoun.

The noun before the relative pronoun and the sentence after it together is called "subject" or (اَلْمُبْتَدَأُ)and the last noun or preposition along with the noun followed by it is called "predicate" or (الْخَبَرُ).

Note:

Read the sentences over and over again to grasp these points properly.

Exercise-1

Translate the following sentences into Arabic:

(1) The car which was stolen last night was mine.

(2) The boy who sits there is your son,

(3) The lady who entered the house is my neighbor.

(4) The student who failed in the exam is from Nepal.

(5) The girl who succeeded in the exam is from India.

Hints: سُرِق (was stolen) , اَلْبَارِحَةُ (last night) , هُنَاكَ (there) , اَلْمَرْأَةُ (the woman) , اَلْجَارَةُ (the neighbour) , فَشِلَ (failed) , نَجَحَتْ (succeeded) .

Exercise-2

Fill in the blanks with suitable relative pronouns.

السَيَّا رَةُ ....وَقَفَتْ أَمَامَ المَكْتَبِ مُعَطَّلَة

الوَلَدُ الطَّوِيْلُ........يَخْرُجُ مِنَ الفَصْلِ إِبْنِي

البَنَاتُ..........يَلْعَبْنَ كُرَةَ السَّلَّةِ صَدِيْقَاتٌ

الرَّجُلاَن........يَتَشَاجَرَانِ مِنَ الهِنْدِ

Hints: وَقَفَتْ (stood) , اَلْمَكْتَبُ (the office) , مُعَطَّلَة (broken down) ,كُرَةُ السَّلَّةِ (basket ball) , تَشَاجَرَ (to quarrel) .

Chapter 26
List of conjugations

A long list of conjugations is being provided in this chapter to help you understand them well. This will also pave the way for speaking Arabic fluently. You just go through the list and memorize them well so you can use them effectively as and when the need arises.

Gender	فِعْلُ الأَمْرِ	المُضَارِعُ المَجْهُوْلُ	المُضَارِعُ المَعْرُوْفُ	المَاضِيْ المَجْهُوْلُ	المَاضِيْ المَعْرُوْفُ	الضَّمَائِرُ
(MS)		يُضْرَبُ	يَضْرِبُ	ضُرِبَ	ضَرَبَ	هُوَ
(MD)		يُضْرَبَانِ	يَضْرِبَانِ	ضُرِبَا	ضَرَبَا	هُمَا
(MP)		يُضْرَبُوْنَ	يَضْرِبُوْنَ	ضُرِبُوْا	ضَرَبُوْا	هُمْ
(FS)		تُضْرَبُ	تَضْرِبُ	ضُرِبَتْ	ضَرَبَتْ	هِيَ
(FD)		تُضْرَبَانِ	تَضْرِبَانِ	ضُرِبَتَا	ضَرَبَتَا	هُمَا
(FP)		يُضْرَبْنَ	يَضْرِبْنَ	ضُرِبْنَ	ضَرَبْنَ	هُنَّ
(MS)	إِضْرِبْ	تُضْرَبُ	تَضْرِبُ	ضُرِبْتَ	ضَرَبْتَ	أَنْتَ
(MD)	إِضْرِبَا	تُضْرَبَانِ	تَضْرِبَانِ	ضُرِبْتُمَا	ضَرَبْتُمَا	أَنْتُمَا
(MP)	إِضْرِبُوْا	تُضْرَبُوْنَ	تَضْرِبُوْنَ	ضُرِبْتُمْ	ضَرَبْتُمْ	أَنْتُمْ
(FS)	إِضْرِبِيْ	تُضْرَبِيْنَ	تَضْرِبِيْنَ	ضُرِبْتِ	ضَرَبْتِ	أَنْتِ
(FD)	إِضْرِبَا	تُضْرَبَانِ	تَضْرِبَانِ	ضُرِبْتُمَا	ضَرَبْتُمَا	أَنْتُمَا
(FP)	إِضْرِبْنَ	تُضْرَبْنَ	تَضْرِبْنَ	ضُرِبْتُنَّ	ضَرَبْتُنَّ	أَنْتُنَّ
(M/F)		أُضْرَبُ	أَضْرِبُ	ضُرِبْتُ	ضَرَبْتُ	أَنَا
(M/F)		نُضْرَبُ	نَضْرِبُ	ضُرِبْنَا	ضَرَبْنَا	نَحْنُ

Verbal noun: ضَرْبٌ\ ضَرَبَانٌ (to beat) .

Doer: ضَارِبٌ

Object: مَضْرُوْبٌ

وَصَلَ (He reached)

Gender	فعلُ الأمْر	المُضارِعُ المَجْهُوْلُ	المُضارِعُ المَعْرُوْفُ	المَاضِيْ المَجْهُوْلُ	المَاضِيْ المَعْرُوْفُ	الضَّمَائِرُ
(MS)		يُوْصَلُ	يَصِلُ	وُصِلَ	وَصَلَ	هُوَ
(MD)		يُوْصَلاَن	يَصِلاَن	وُصِلاَ	وَصَلاَ	هُمَا
(MP)		يُوْصَلُوْنَ	يَصِلُوْنَ	وُصِلُوْا	وَصَلُوْا	هُمْ
(FS)		تُوْصَلُ	تَصِلُ	وُصِلَتْ	وَصَلَتْ	هِيَ
(FD)		تُوْصَلاَن	تَصِلاَن	وُصِلَتَا	وَصَلَتَا	هُمَا
(FP)		يُوْصَلْنَ	يَصِلْنَ	وُصِلْنَ	وَصَلْنَ	هُنَّ
(MS)	صِلْ	تُوْصَلُ	تَصِلُ	وُصِلْتَ	وَصَلْتَ	أَنْتَ
(MD)	صِلاَ	تُوْصَلاَن	تَصِلاَن	وُصِلْتُمَا	وَصَلْتُمَا	أَنْتُمَا
(MP)	صِلُوْا	تُوْصَلُوْنَ	تَصِلُوْنَ	وُصِلْتُمْ	وَصَلْتُمْ	أَنْتُمْ
(FS)	صِلِيْ	تُوْصَلِيْنَ	تَصِلِيْنَ	وُصِلْتِ	وَصَلْتِ	أَنْتِ
(FD)	صِلاَ	تُوْصَلاَن	تَصِلاَن	وُصِلْتُمَا	وَصَلْتُمَا	أَنْتُمَا
(FP)	صِلْنَ	تُوْصَلْنَ	تَصِلْنَ	وُصِلْتُنَّ	وَصَلْتُنَّ	أَنْتُنَّ
(M/S)		أُوْصَلُ	أَصِلُ	وُصِلْتُ	وَصَلْتُ	أَنَا
(M/S)		نُوْصَلُ	نَصِلُ	وُصِلْنَا	وَصَلْنَا	نَحْنُ

Verbal noun: وَصْلٌ \ صِلَة (to reach) .

Doer: وَاصِلٌ

Object: مَوْصُوْلٌ

أخَذَ (He took)

Gender	فِعْلُ الْأمر	اَلمُضَارِعُ المَجْهُوْلُ	اَلمُضَارِعُ المَعْرُوْفُ	اَلمَاضِي المَجْهُوْلُ	اَلمَاضِيْ المَعْرُوْفُ	اَلضَّمَائِرُ
(MS) *		يُؤْخَذُ	يَأْخُذُ	أُخِذَ	أَخَذَ	هُوَ
(MD)		يُؤْخَذَانِ	يَأْخُذَانِ	أُخِذَا	أَخَذَا	هُمَا
(MP)		يُؤْخَذُوْنَ	يَأْخُذُوْنَ	أُخِذُوْا	أَخَذُوْا	هُمْ
(FS)		تُؤْخَذُ	تَأْخُذُ	أُخِذَتْ	أَخَذَتْ	هِيَ
(FD)		تُؤْخَذَانِ	تَأْخُذَانِ	أُخِذَتَا	أَخَذَتَا	هُمَا
(FP)		يُؤْخَذْنَ	يَأْخُذْنَ	أُخِذْنَ	أَخَذْنَ	هُنَّ
(MS)	خُذْ	تُؤْخَذُ	تَأْخُذُ	أُخِذْتَ	أَخَذْتَ	أَنْتَ
(MD)	خُذَا	تُؤْخَذَانِ	تَأْخُذَانِ	أُخِذْتُمَا	أَخَذْتُمَا	أَنْتُمَا
(MP)	خُذُوْا	تُؤْخَذُوْنَ	تَأْخُذُوْنَ	أُخِذْتُمْ	أَخَذْتُمْ	أَنْتُمْ
(FS)	خُذِيْ	تُؤْخَذِيْنَ	تَأْخُذِيْنَ	أُخِذْتِ	أَخَذْتِ	أَنْتِ
(FD)	خُذَا	تُؤْخَذَانِ	تَأْخُذَانِ	أُخِذْتُمَا	أَخَذْتُمَا	أَنْتُمَا
(FP)	خُذْنَ	تُؤْخَذْنَ	تَأْخُذْنَ	أُخِذْتُنَّ	أَخَذْتُنَّ	أَنْتُنَّ
(M/F)		أُوْخَذُ	آخُذُ	أُخِذْتُ	أَخَذْتُ	أَنَا
(M/F)		نُؤْخَذُ	نَأْخُذُ	أُخِذْنَا	أَخَذْنَا	نَحْنُ

Verbal noun: أَخْذٌ (to take) .
Doer: آخِذٌ
Object: مَأْخُوْذٌ

- This symbolizes the gender. MS stands for Masculine Singular and FS stands for Feminine Singular. You should keep these symbols in mind while going through this book.

قَالَ (He said)

Gender	فِعْلُ الأَمْر	اَلمُضَارِعُ اَلمَجْهُوْلُ	اَلمُضَارِعُ اَلمَعْرُوْفُ	اَلمَاضِيْ اَلمَجْهُوْلُ	اَلمَاضِيْ اَلمَعْرُوْفُ	اَلضَّمَائِرُ
(MS)		يُقَالُ	يَقُوْلُ	قِيْلَ	قَالَ	هُوَ
(MD)		يُقَالَانِ	يَقُوْلَانِ	قِيْلَا	قَالَا	هُمَا
(MP)		يُقَالُوْنَ	يَقُوْلُوْنَ	قِيْلُوْا	قَالُوْا	هُمْ
(FS)		تُقَالُ	تَقُوْلُ	قِيْلَتْ	قَالَتْ	هِيَ
(FD)		تُقَالَانِ	تَقُوْلَانِ	قِيْلَتَا	قَالَتَا	هُمَا
(FP)		يُقَلْنَ	يَقُلْنَ	قِلْنَ	قُلْنَ	هُنَّ
(MS)	قُلْ	تُقَالُ	تَقُوْلُ	قِلْتَ	قُلْتَ	أَنْتَ
(MD)	قُوْلَا	تُقَالَانِ	تَقُوْلَانِ	قِلْتُمَا	قُلْتُمَا	أَنْتُمَا
(MP)	قُوْلُوْا	تُقَالُوْنَ	تَقُوْلُوْنَ	قِلْتُمْ	قُلْتُمْ	أَنْتُمْ
(FS)	قُوْلِيْ	تُقَالِيْنَ	تَقُوْلِيْنَ	قِلْتِ	قُلْتِ	أَنْتِ
(FD)	قُوْلَا	تُقَالَانِ	تَقُوْلَانِ	قِلْتُمَا	قُلْتُمَا	أَنْتُمَا
(FP)	قُلْنَ	تُقَلْنَ	تَقُلْنَ	قِلْتُنَّ	قُلْتُنَّ	أَنْتُنَّ
(M/F)		أُقَالُ	أَقُوْلُ	قِلْتُ	قُلْتُ	أَنَا
(M/F)		نُقَالُ	نَقُوْلُ	قِلْنَا	قُلْنَا	نَحْنُ

Verbal noun: مَقَالَةٌ /مَقَالٌ /قَوْلَةٌ /قَوْلٌ (to say) .

Doer: قَائِلٌ

Object: مَقُوُوْلٌ /مَقُوْلٌ

فرَّ (He fled)

Gender	فِعْلُ الْأمْر	المُضَارِعُ المَجْهُوْلُ	المُضَارِعُ المَعْرُوْفُ	المَاضِيْ المَجْهُوْلُ	المَاضِيْ المَعْرُوْفُ	الضَّمَائِرُ
(MS)		يُفَرُّ	يَفِرُّ	فُرَّ	فرَّ	هُوَ
(MD)		يُفَرَّان	يَفِرَّان	فُرَّا	فرَّا	هُمَا
(MP)		يُفَرُّوْنَ	يَفِرُّوْنَ	فُرُّوْا	فرُّوْا	هُمْ
(FS)		تُفَرُّ	تَفِرُّ	فُرَّتْ	فرَّتْ	هِيَ
(FD)		تُفَرَّان	تَفِرَّان	فُرَّتَا	فرَّتَا	هُمَا
(FP)		يُفْرَرْنَ	يَفِرَرْنَ	فُرِرْنَ	فرَرْنَ	هُنَّ
(MS)	فِرَّ	تُفَرُّ	تَفِرُّ	فُرِرْتَ	فرَرْتَ	أنْتَ
(MD)	فِرَّا	تُفَرَّان	تَفِرَّان	فُرِرْتُمَا	فرَرْتُمَا	أنْتُمَا
(MP)	فِرُّوْا	تُفَرُّوْنَ	تَفِرُّوْنَ	فُرِرْتُمْ	فرَرْتُمْ	أنْتُمْ
(FS)	فِرِّي	تُفَرِّيْنَ	تَفِرِّيْنَ	فُرِرْتِ	فرَرْتِ	أنْتِ
(FD)	فِرَّا	تُفَرَّان	تَفِرَّان	فُرِرْتُمَا	فرَرْتُمَا	أنْتُمَا
(FP)	إفْرِرْنَ	تُفْرَرْنَ	تَفْرِرْنَ	فُرِرْتُنَّ	فرَرْتُنَّ	أنْتُنَّ
(M/F)		أفَرُّ	أفِرُّ	فُرِرْتُ	فرَرْتُ	أنَا
(M/F)		نُفَرُّ	نَفِرُّ	فُرِرْنَا	فرَرْنَا	نَحْنُ

Verbal noun: مَفَرٌّ /فِرَارٌ /فرٌّ (to flee) .
Doer: فَارٌّ
Object: مَفْرُوْرٌ

دَعَا (He invited/ he called out)

Gender	فِعْلُ الْأَمْر	الْمُضَارِعُ الْمَجْهُوْلُ	الْمُضَارِعُ الْمَعْرُوْفُ	الْمَاضِيْ الْمَجْهُوْلُ	الْمَاضِي الْمَعْرُوْفُ	الضَّمَائِرُ
(MS)		يُدْعَيْ	يَدْعُوْ	دُعِيَ	دَعَا	هُوَ
(MD)		يُدْعَيَان	يَدْعُوان	دُعِيَا	دَعَوَا	هُمَا
(MP)		يُدْعَوْنَ	يَدْعُوْنَ	دُعُوْا	دَعَوْا	هُمْ
(FS)		تُدْعَيْ	تَدْعُوْ	دُعِيَتْ	دَعَتْ	هِيَ
(FD)		تُدْعَيَان	تَدْعُوَان	دُعِيَتَا	دَعَتَا	هُمَا
(FP)		يُدْعَيْنَ	يَدْعُوْنَ	دُعِيْنَ	دَعَوْنَ	هُنَّ
(MS)	أُدْعُ	تُدْعَيْ	تَدْعُوْ	دُعِيْتَ	دَعَوْتَ	أَنْتَ
(MD)	أُدْعُوَا	تُدْعَيَان	تَدْعُوَان	دُعِيْتُمَا	دَعَوْتُمَا	أَنْتُمَا
(MP)	أُدْعُوْا	تُدْعَوْنَ	تَدْعُوْنَ	دُعِيْتُمْ	دَعَوْتُمْ	أَنْتُمْ
(FS)	أُدْعِيْ	تُدْعَيْنَ	تَدْعِيْنَ	دُعِيْتِ	دعَوْتِ	أَنْتِ
(FD)	أُدْعُوَا	تُدْعَيَان	تَدْعُوَان	دُعِيْتُمَا	دَعَوْتُمَا	أَنْتُمَا
(FP)	أُدْعُوْنَ	تُدْعَيْنَ	تَدْعُوْنَ	دُعِيْتُنَّ	دَعَوْتُنَّ	أَنْتُنَّ
(M/F)		أُدْعَيْ	أَدْعُوْ	دُعِيْتُ	دَعَوْتُ	أَنَا
(M/F)		نُدْعَيْ	نَدْعُوْ	دُعِيْنَا	دَعَوْنَا	نَحْنُ

Verbal noun: دُعَاءٌ\ دَعْوَةٌ (to invite/ to call out)
Doer: دَاعٍ
Object: مَدْعُوٌّ

بَاعَ (He sold)

Gender	فِعْلُ الْأَمْرِ	الْمُضَارِعُ الْمَجْهُوْلُ	الْمُضَارِعُ الْمَعْرُوْفُ	الْمَاضِي الْمَجْهُوْلُ	الْمَاضِيْ الْمَعْرُوْفُ	الضَّمَائِرُ
(MS)		يُبَاعُ	يَبِيْعُ	بِيْعَ	بَاعَ	هُوَ
(MD)		يُبَاعَان	يَبِيْعَان	بِيْعَا	بَاعَا	هُمَا
(MP)		يُبَاعُوْنَ	يَبِيْعُوْنَ	بِيْعُوْا	بَاعُوْا	هُمْ
(FS)		تُبَاعُ	تَبِيْعُ	بِيْعَتْ	بَاعَتْ	هِيَ
(FD)		تُبَاعَان	تَبِيْعَان	بِيْعَتَا	بَاعَتَا	هُمَا
(FP)		يُبَعْنَ	يَبِعْنَ	بِعْنَ	بِعْنَ	هُنَّ
(MS)	بِعْ	تُبَاعُ	تَبِيْعُ	بِعْتَ	بِعْتَ	أَنْتَ
(MD)	بِيْعَا	تُبَاعَان	تَبِيْعَان	بِعْتُمَا	بِعْتُمَا	أَنْتُمَا
(MP)	بِيْعُوْا	تُبَاعُوْنَ	تَبِيْعُوْنَ	بِعْتُمْ	بِعْتُمْ	أَنْتُمْ
(FS)	بِيْعِيْ	تُبَاعِيْنَ	تَبِيْعِيْنَ	بِعْتِ	بِعْتِ	أَنْتِ
(FD)	بِيْعَا	تُبَاعَان	تَبِيْعَان	بِعْتُمَا	بِعْتُمَا	أَنْتُمَا
(FP)	بِعْنَ	تُبَعْنَ	تَبِعْنَ	بِعْتُنَّ	بِعْتُنَّ	أَنْتُنَّ
(M/F)		أُبَاعُ	أَبِيْعُ	بِعْتُ	بِعْتُ	أَنَا
(M/F)		نُبَاعُ	نَبِيْعُ	بِعْنَا	بِعْنَا	نَحْنُ

Verbal noun: بَيْعٌ \ مَبِيْعٌ (to sell)
Doer: بَائِعٌ
Object: مَبِيْعٌ \ مَبْيُوْعٌ

جَاءَ (He came)

Gender	فِعْلُ الْأَمْر	اَلْمُضَارِعُ الْمَجْهُوْلُ	اَلْمُضَارِعُ الْمَعْرُوْفُ	اَلْمَاضِيْ الْمَجْهُوْلُ	اَلْمَاضِيْ الْمَعْرُوْفُ	اَلضَّمَائِرُ
(MS)		يُجَاءُ	يَجِيءُ	جِيءَ	جَاءَ	هُوَ
(MD)		يُجَاءَانِ	يَجِيئَانِ	جِيئَا	جَاءَا	هُمَا
(MP)		يُجَاؤُوْنَ	يَجِيئُوْنَ	جِيئُوْا	جَاؤُوْا	هُمْ
(FS)		تُجَاءُ	تَجِيءُ	جِيئَتْ	جَاءَتْ	هِيَ
(FD)		تُجَاءَانِ	تَجِيئَانِ	جِيئَتَا	جَاءَتَا	هُمَا
(FP)		يُجَأْنَ	يَجِئْنَ	جِئْنَ	جِئْنَ	هُنَّ
(MS)	جِئْ	تُجَاءُ	تَجِيءُ	جِئْتَ	جِئْتَ	أَنْتَ
(MD)	جِيئَا	تُجَاءَانِ	تَجِيئَانِ	جِئْتُمَا	جِئْتُمَا	أَنْتُمَا
(MP)	جِيئُوْا	تُجَاؤُوْنَ	تَجِيئُوْنَ	جِئْتُمْ	جِئْتُمْ	أَنْتُمْ
(FS)	جِيئِي	تُجَائِيْنَ	تَجِيئِيْنَ	جِئْتِ	جِئْتِ	أَنْتِ
(FD)	جِيئَا	تُجَاءَانِ	تَجِيئَانِ	جِئْتُمَا	جِئْتُمَا	أَنْتُمَا
(FP)	جِئْنَ	تُجَأْنَ	تَجِئْنَ	جِئْتُنَّ	جِئْتُنَّ	أَنْتُنَّ
(M/F)		أُجَاءُ	أَجِيءُ	جِئْتُ	جِئْتُ	أَنَا
(M/F)		نُجَاءُ	نَجِيءُ	جِئْنَا	جِئْنَا	نَحْنُ

Verbal Noun: جَيْئًا\ مَجِيءٌ (to come)

Doer: جَاءٍ

Object: مَجِيءٌ

أَتَي (He came)

Gender	فِعْلُ الْأَمْر	الْمُضَارِعُ الْمَجْهُوْلُ	الْمُضَارِعُ الْمَعْرُوْفُ	الْمَاضِيْ الْمَجْهُوْلُ	الْمَاضِيْ الْمَعْرُوْفُ	الضَّمَائِرُ
(MS)		يُؤْتَيْ	يَأْتِيْ	أُتِيَ	أَتَي	هُوَ
(MD)		يُؤْتَيَان	يَأْتِيَان	أُتِيَا	أَتَيَا	هُمَا
(MP)		يُؤْتَوْنَ	يَأْتُوْنَ	أُتُوْا	أَتَوْا	هُمْ
(FS)		تُؤْتَيْ	تَأْتِيْ	أُتِيَتْ	أَتَتْ	هِيَ
(FD)		تُؤْتَيَان	تَأْتِيَان	أُتِيَتَا	أَتَتَا	هُمَا
(FP)		يُؤْتَيْنَ	يَأْتِيْنَ	أُتِيْنَ	أَتَيْنَ	هُنَّ
(MS)	إِئْتِ,	تُؤْتَيْ	تَأْتِيْ	أُتِيْتَ	أَتَيْتَ	أَنْتَ
(MD)	إِيْتِ	تُؤْتَيَان	تَأْتِيَان	أُتِيْتُمَا	أَتَيْتُمَا	أَنْتُمَا
(MP)	إِئْتِيَا	تُؤْتَوْنَ	تَأْتُوْنَ	أُتِيْتُمْ	أَتَيْتُمْ	أَنْتُمْ
	إِئْتُوْا					
(FS)	إِئْتِيْ	تُؤْتَيْنَ	تَأْتِيْنَ	أُتِيْتِ	أَتَيْتِ	أَنْتِ
(FD)	إِئْتِيَا	تُؤْتَيَان	تَأْتِيَان	أُتِيْتُمَا	أَتَيْتُمَا	أَنْتُمَا
(FP)	إِئْتِيْنَ	تُؤْتَيْنَ	تَأْتِيْنَ	أُتِيْتُنَّ	أَتَيْتُنَّ	أَنْتُنَّ
(M/F)		أُوْتَيْ	آتِيْ	أُتِيْتُ	أَتَيْتُ	أَنَا
(M/F)		نُؤْتَيْ	نَأْتِيْ	أُتِيْنَا	أَتَيْنَا	نَحْنُ

Verbal noun: أَتْيٌ\ إِتْيَانٌ (to come)
Doer: آتٍ
Object: مَأْتِيٌّ

طَوَيْ (He wrapped up)

Gender	فِعْلُ الْأمْر	اَلْمُضَارِعُ الْمَجْهُوْلُ	اَلْمُضَارِعُ الْمَعْرُوْفُ	اَلْمَاضِيْ الْمَجْهُوْلُ	اَلْمَاضِيْ الْمَعْرُوْفُ	اَلضَّمَائِرُ
(MS)		يُطْوَيْ	يَطْوِيْ	طُوِيَ	طَوَيْ	هُوَ
(MD)		يُطْوَيَان	يَطْوِيَان	طُوِيَا	طَوَيَا	هُمَا
(MP)		يُطْوَوْنَ	يَطْوُوْنَ	طُوُوْا	طَوَوْا	هُمْ
(FS)		تُطْوَيْ	تَطْوِيْ	طُوِيَتْ	طَوَتْ	هِيَ
(FD)		تُطْوَيَان	تَطْوِيَان	طُوِيَتَا	طَوَتَا	هُمَا
(FP)		يُطْوَيْنَ	يَطْوِيْنَ	طُوِيْنَ	طَوَيْنَ	هُنَّ
(MS)	إِطْوِ	تُطْوَيْ	تَطْوِيْ	طُوِيْتَ	طَوَيْتَ	أَنْتَ
(MD)	إِطْوِيَا	تُطْوَيَان	تَطْوِيَان	طُوِيْتُمَا	طَوَيْتُمَا	أَنْتُمَا
(MP)	إِطْوُوْا	تُطْوَوْنَ	تَطْوُوْنَ	طُوِيْتُمْ	طَوَيْتُمْ	أَنْتُمْ
(MS)	إِطْوِيْ	تُطْوَيْنَ	تَطْوِيْنَ	طُوِيْتِ	طَوَيْتِ	أَنْتِ
(MD)	إِطْوِيَا	تُطْوَيَان	تَطْوِيَان	طُوِيْتُمَا	طَوَيْتُمَا	أَنْتُمَا
(MP)	إِطْوِيْنَ	تُطْوَيْنَ	تَطْوِيْنَ	طُوِيْتُنَّ	طَوَيْتُنَّ	أَنْتُنَّ
(M/F)		أُطْوَيْ	أَطْوِيْ	طُوِيْتُ	طَوَيْتُ	أَنَا
(M/F)		نُطْوَيْ	نَطْوِيْ	طُوِيْنَا	طَوَيْنَا	نَحْنُ

Verbal noun: طَيٌّ (to wrap up/ to roll)
Doer: طَاوٍ
Object: مَطْوِيٌّ

وَفَيْ (He fulfilled)

Gender	فِعْلُ الْأَمْرِ	اَلْمُضَارِعُ الْمَجْهُوْلُ	اَلْمُضَارِعُ الْمَعْرُوْفُ	اَلْمَاضِيْ الْمَجْهُوْلُ	اَلْمَاضِيْ الْمَعْرُوْفُ	اَلضَّمَائِرُ
(MS)		يُوْفَيْ	يَفِيْ	وُفِيَ	وَفَيْ	هُوَ
(MD)		يُوْفَيَان	يَفَان	وُفِيَا	وَفَيَا	هُمَا
(MP)		يُوْفَوْنَ	يَفَوْنَ	وُفُوْا	وَفَوْا	هُمْ
(FS)		تُوْفَيْ	تَفِيْ	وُفِيَتْ	وَفَتْ	هِيَ
(FD)		تُوْفَيَان	تَفِيَان	وُفِيَتَا	وَفَتَا	هُمَا
(FP)		يُوْفَيْنَ	يَفَيْنَ	وُفِيْنَ	وَفَيْنَ	هُنَّ
(MS)	فِ	تُوْفَيْ	تَفِيْ	وُفِيْتَ	وَفَيْتَ	أَنْتَ
(MD)	فِيَا	تُوْفَيَان	تَفِيَان	وُفِيْتُمَا	وَفَيْتُمَا	أَنْتُمَا
(MP)	فُوْا	تُوْفَوْنَ	تَفَوْنَ	وُفِيْتُمْ	وَفَيْتُمْ	أَنْتُمْ
(FS)	فِيْ	تُوْفَيْنَ	تَفِيْنَ	وُفِيْتِ	وَفَيْتِ	أَنْتِ
(FD)	فِيَا	تُوْفَيَان	تَفِيَان	وُفِيْتُمَا	وَفَيْتُمَا	أَنْتُمَا
(FP)	فِيْنَ	تُوْفَيْن	تَفِيْنَ	وُفِيْتُنَّ	وَفَيْتُنَّ	أَنْتُنَّ
(M/F)		أُوْفَيْ	أَفِيْ	وُفِيْتُ	وَفَيْتُ	أَنَا
(M/F)		نُوْفَيْ	نَفِيْ	وُفِيْنَا	وَفَيْنَا	نَحْنُ

Verbal noun: وَفَاءٌ (to fulfill)
Doer: وَافٍ
Object: مَوْفِيٌّ

عَضَّ (He bit)

Gender	فِعْلُ الْأَمْرِ	الْمُضَارِعُ الْمَجْهُوْلُ	الْمُضَارِعُ الْمَعْرُوْفُ	الْمَاضِيْ الْمَجْهُوْلُ	الْمَاضِيْ الْمَعْرُوْفُ	الضَّمَائِرُ
(MS)		يُعَضُّ	يَعَضُّ	عُضَّ	عَضَّ	هُوَ
(MD)		يُعَضَّان	يَعَضَّان	عُضَّا	عَضَّا	هُمَا
(MP)		يُعَضُّوْنَ	يَعَضُّوْنَ	عُضُّوْا	عَضُّوْا	هُمْ
(FS)		تُعَضُّ	تَعَضُّ	عُضَّتْ	عَضَّتْ	هِيَ
(FD)		تُعَضَّان	تَعَضَّان	عُضَّتَا	عَضَّتَا	هُمَا
(FP)		يُعْضَضْنَ	يَعْضَضْنَ	عُضِضْنَ	عَضَضْنَ	هُنَّ
(MS)	عَضَّ	تُعَضُّ	تَعَضُّ	عُضِضْتَ	عَضَضْتَ	أَنْتَ
(MD)	عَضَّا	تُعَضَّان	تَعَضَّان	عُضِضْتُمَا	عَضَضْتُمَا	أَنْتُمَا
(MP)	عَضُّوْا	تُعَضُّوْنَ	تَعَضُّوْنَ	عُضِضْتُمْ	عَضَضْتُمْ	أَنْتُمْ
(FS)	عَضِّيْ	تُعَضِّيْنَ	تَعَضِّيْنَ	عُضِضْتِ	عَضَضْتِ	أَنْتِ
(FD)	عَضَّا	تُعَضَّان	تَعَضَّان	عُضِضْتُمَا	عَضَضْتُمَا	أَنْتُمَا
(FP)	اِعْضَضْنَ	تُعْضَضْنَ	تَعْضَضْنَ	عُضِضْتُنَّ	عَضَضْتُنَّ	أَنْتُنَّ
(M/F)		أُعَضُّ	أَعَضُّ	عُضِضْتُ	عَضَضْتُ	أَنَا
(M/F)		نُعَضُّ	نَعَضُّ	عُضِضْنَا	عَضَضْنَا	نَحْنُ

Verbal noun: عَضٌّ\ عَضِيْضٌ (to bite)
Doer: عَاضٌّ
Object: مَعْضُوْضٌ

سَأَلَ (He said)

Gender	فِعْلُ الأمْرِ	المُضَارِعُ المَجْهُوْلُ	المُضَارِعُ المَعْرُوْفُ	المَاضِيْ المَجْهُوْلُ	المَاضِيْ المَعْرُوْفُ	الضَّمَائِرُ
(MS)		يُسْأَلُ	يَسْأَلُ	سُئِلَ	سَأَلَ	هُوَ
(MD)		يُسْأَلَان	يَسْأَلَان	سُئِلا	سَأَلا	هُمَا
(MP)		يُسْأَلُوْنَ	يَسْأَلُوْنَ	سُئِلُوْا	سَأَلُوْا	هُمْ
(FS)		تُسْأَلُ	تَسْأَلُ	سُئِلَتْ	سَأَلَتْ	هِيَ
(FD)		تُسْأَلان	تَسْأَلان	سُئِلَتَا	سَأَلَتَا	هُمَا
(FP)		يُسْأَلنَ	يَسْأَلنَ	سُئِلنَ	سَأَلنَ	هُنَّ
(MS)	إسْأَلْ\	تُسْأَلُ	تَسْأَلُ	سُئِلتَ	سَأَلتَ	أنْتَ
(MD)	سَلْ	تُسْأَلان	تَسْأَلان	سُئِلتُمَا	سَأَلتُمَا	أنتُمَا
(MP)	إسْألا	تُسْأَلُوْنَ	تَسْأَلُوْنَ	سُئِلتُمْ	سَأَلتُمْ	أنتُمْ
	إسْأَلُوْا					
(FS)	إسْأَلِي	تُسْأَلِيْنَ	تَسْأَلِيْنَ	سُئِلتِ	سَأَلتِ	أنتِ
(FD)	إسْألا	تُسْأَلان	تَسْأَلان	سُئِلتُمَا	سَأَلتُمَا	أنتُمَا
(FP)	إسْأَلنَ	تُسْأَلنَ	تَسْأَلنَ	سُئِلتُنَّ	سَأَلتُنَّ	أنتُنَّ
(M/F)		أُسْأَلُ	أَسْأَلُ	سُئِلتُ	سَأَلتُ	أنَا
(M/F)		نُسْأَلُ	نَسْأَلُ	سُئِلنَا	سَأَلنَا	نَحْنُ

Verbal noun: سُؤَالٌ\ مَسْئَلَة (to ask)
Doer: سَائِلٌ
Object: مَسْئُوْلٌ

رأي (He saw)

Gender	فِعْلُ الْأمْرِ	المُضَارِعُ المَجْهُوْلُ	المُضَارِعُ المَعْرُوْفُ	المَاضِيْ المَجْهُوْلُ	المَاضِي المَعْرُوْفُ	الضَّمَائِرُ
(MS)		يُرَي	يَرَي	رُئِيَ	رَأَيْ	هُوَ
(MD)		يُرَيَانِ	يَرَيَانِ	رُئِيَا	رَأَيَا	هُمَا
(MP)		يُرَوْنَ	يَرَوْنَ	رُؤُوْا	رَأَوْا	هُمْ
(FS)		تُرَي	تَرَي	رُئِيَتْ	رَأَتْ	هِيَ
(FD)		تُرَيَانِ	تَرَيَانِ	رُئِيَا	رَأَتَا	هُمَا
(FP)		يُرَيْنَ	يَرَيْنَ	رُئِيْنَ	رَأَيْنَ	هُنَّ
(MS)	رَ	تُرَي	تَرَي	رُئِيْتَ	رَأَيْتَ	أنْتَ
(MD)	رَيَا	تُرَيَانِ	تَرَيَانِ	رُئِيْتُمَا	رَأَيْتُمَا	أنْتُمَا
(MP)	رَوْا	تُرَوْنَ	تَرَوْنَ	رُئِيْتُمْ	رَأَيْتُمْ	أنْتُمْ
(FS)	رَيْ	تُرَيْنَ	تَرَيْنَ	رُئِيْتِ	رَأَيْتِ	أنْتِ
(FD)	رَيَا	تُرَيَانِ	تَرَيَانِ	رُئِيْتُمَا	رَأَيْتُمَا	أنْتُمَا
(FM)	رَيْنَ	تُرَيْنَ	تَرَيْنَ	رُئِيْتُنَّ	رَأَيْتُنَّ	أنْتُنَّ
(M/F)		أُرَيْ	أَرَيْ	رُئِيْتُ	رَأَيْتُ	أنَا
(M/F)		نُرَي	نَرَي	رُئِيْنَا	رَأَيْنَا	نَحْنُ

Verbal noun: رُؤْيَةٌ\ رَاءَةٌ (to see)
Doer: رَاءٍ (رَائِيٌ)
Object: مَرْئِيٌّ

وَضَعَ (He put)

Gender	فِعْلُ الْأمْر	اَلْمُضَارِعُ الْمَجْهُوْلُ	اَلْمُضَارِعُ الْمَعْرُوْفُ	اَلْمَاضِيْ الْمَجْهُوْلُ	اَلْمَاضِيْ الْمَعْرُوْفُ	اَلضَّمَائِرُ
(MS)		يُوْضَعُ	يَضَعُ	وُضِعَ	وَضَعَ	هُوَ
(MD)		يُوْضَعَانِ	يَضَعَانِ	وُضِعَا	وَضَعَا	هُمَا
(MP)		يُوْضَعُوْنَ	يَضَعُوْنَ	وُضِعُوْا	وَضَعُوْا	هُمْ
(FS)		تُوْضَعُ	تَضَعُ	وُضِعَتْ	وَضَعَتْ	هِيَ
(FD)		تُوْضَعَانِ	تَضَعَانِ	وُضِعَتَا	وَضَعَتَا	هُمَا
(FP)		يُوْضَعْنَ	يَضَعْنَ	وُضِعْنَ	وَضَعْنَ	هُنَّ
(MS)	ضَعْ	تُوْضَعُ	تَضَعُ	وُضِعْتَ	وَضَعْتَ	أنْتَ
(MD)	ضَعَا	تُوْضَعَانِ	تَضَعَانِ	وُضِعْتُمَا	وَضَعْتُمَا	أنْتُمَا
(MP)	ضَعُوْا	تُوْضَعُوْنَ	تَضَعُوْنَ	وُضِعْتُمْ	وَضَعْتُمْ	أنْتُمْ
(FS)	ضَعِي	تُوْضَعِيْنَ	تَضَعِيْنَ	وُضِعْتِ	وَضَعْتِ	أنْتِ
(FD)	ضَعَا	تُوْضَعَانِ	تَضَعَانِ	وُضِعْتُمَا	وَضَعْتُمَا	أنْتُمَا
(FP)	ضَعْنَ	تُوْضَعْنَ	تَضَعْنَ	وُضِعْتُنَّ	وَضَعْتُنَّ	أنْتُنَّ
(M/F)		أُوْضَعُ	أضَعُ	وُضِعْتُ	وَضَعْتُ	أنَا
(M/F)		نُوْضَعُ	نَضَعُ	وُضِعْنَا	وَضَعْنَا	نَحْنُ

Vebal noun: وَضْعٌ (to put)
Doer: وَاضِعٌ
Object: مَوْضُوْعٌ

Chapter 27
Exceptions in Arabic Grammar

(A) Five nouns

There are some exceptions in Arabic grammar which you must understand to avoid any mistake while writing or speaking. One of such exceptions is called "Five Nouns" or (اَلْأَسْمَاءُ الخَمْسَةُ). These Five nouns of Arabic are:

Five nouns	اَلْأَسْمَاءُ الخَمْسَةُ
Father	أَبٌ
Brother	أَخٌ
Mouth	فَمٌ
In-law	حَمٌ
(one who) has something	ذُوْ

To understand what is exceptional about these nouns just go through the model sentences given in the below column.

When did your brother come?	مَتَي جَاءَ أَخُوْكَ؟
I saw your brother at the airport.	رَأَيْتُ أَخَاكَ فِيْ المَطَار
What happened to your brother?	مَاذَا حَدَثَ بِأَخِيْكَ؟
What is that in your mouth?	مَا هُوَ بِفِيْكَ؟
His mouth is wide.	فُوْه وَاسِعٌ
I found his mouth open.	وَجَدْتُ فَاهُ مَفْتُوْحاً

Five star hotel.	الْفُنْدُقُ ذُوْ النُّجُوْمِ الْخَمْسَةِ
I met with a man of repute.	لَقِيْتُ رَجُلاً ذَا شُهْرَةٍ
I got past a well-off man.	مَرَرْتُ بِرُجُلٍ ذِيْ مَالٍ
His father paid the bill.	دَفَعَ أَبُوْهُ الفَاتُوْرَةَ
The Government invited his father to deliver the lecture.	دَعَتِ الحُكُوْمَةُ أَبَاهُ لِإلقاء المُحَاضَرَةِ
My friend visited London with his father.	زَارَ صَدِيْقِيْ لَنْدَنَ مَعَ أَبِيْهِ

If you look at the above examples you will realize that these nouns are exceptional because their vowel mark "Damma" becomes وَاو, their "Fat-ha" becomes اَلِفٌ and their "Kas-ra" becomes يَاءٌ.
ذُوْ and all other nouns of this group are always used as "Al-mu-dha-fu" and وَاوُ of ذُوْ also changes into اَلِف and يَاء and becomes ذَا,ذِي as per its position in the sentence.
The feminine of ذُوْ is ذَاتُ
The feminine of ذَا is ذَاتَ
The feminine of ذِيْ is ذَاتِ.

(B) Feminine without round (ة)

You have read that feminine noun in Arabic is made by suffixing round ta (ة). But there are some nouns in Arabic which are used as feminine despite having no round ta (ة). This is because the Arabs use these words as feminine only. These nouns are as below:

The palm The ear	الكَفُّ الْأُذُنُ	The fire The war	النَّارُ الحَرْبُ
The finger The wine	الإِصْبَعُ الخَمْرُ	The air The earth	الرِّيْحُ الْأَرْضُ
The leg	الرِّجْلُ	The sun	الشَّمْسُ

The foot	القَدَمُ	The glass	الكَأسُ
The arm The hand	الذِّرَاعُ اليَدُ	The house The eye	الدَّارُ العَيْنُ

Such nouns do not confine to the above examples alone. There are more than the above mentioned nouns about which you will learn during the course of your study.

Look at the use of some of these words:

The fire burns in the house.	تَضْطَرِمُ النَّارُ فِي البَيْتِ
The war killed thousands.	قَتَلَتِ الحَرْبُ آلافاً
The wind is hard.	الرِّيْحُ شَدِيْدَةٌ
The earth is dry.	الأَرْضُ يَابِسَةٌ
The sun is rising.	الشَّمْسُ طَالِعَةٌ
The glass is filled with the tea.	الكَاسُ مَلِيْئَةٌ بِالشَّايِ
The house is big.	الدَّارُ كَبِيْرَةٌ
The eye is wide.	العَيْنُ وَاسِعَةٌ
The palm is soft.	الكَفُّ نَاعِمَةٌ
The ear is long.	الأُذُنُ طَوِيْلَةٌ
The finger is short.	الإِصْبَعُ قَصِيْرَةٌ
The wine is old.	الخَمْرُ عَتِيْقَةٌ
The leg is broken.	الرِّجْلُ مَكْسُوْرَةٌ
The step is heavy.	القَدَمُ ثَقِيْلَةٌ
The arm is long.	الذِّرَاعُ طَوِيْلَةٌ
The right hand.	اليَدُ اليُمْنَى
The left hand.	اليَدُ اليُسْرَى

(C) Declinable and indeclinable nouns

There are two kinds of noun in Arabic in terms of accepting vowel marks on its last letter:

One which carries vowel marks on its last letter as per its position in a sentence. That means that such nouns can accept all the vowel marks be it damma, fatha or kasra and are called declinable or المُعْرَبُ in Arabic. Examples are:

The bridge is long. The kind built the bridge. I walked on the bridge.	الجِسْرُ طوِيْلٌ بَنَي المَلِكُ الجِسْرَ مَشَيْتُ عَلَي الجِسْرِ

You can see in the above examples that (الجِسْرُ)is a declinable noun (الإِسْمُ المُعْرَبُ)which has accepted all the three vowels as per its position in the sentence.

However, a noun or a pronoun which does not accept all the three vowel marks on its last letter is called indeclinable or (المَبْنِي). These are:

(1) Demonstrative pronouns

(2) Pronouns

(3) Particles of interrogation and many others.

Examples:

هُوَ, هُمَا, هُمْ, هُنَّ, أَنْتَ, أَنْتُمَا, أَنْتُمْ, أَنْتُنَّ, هَلْ, أ, أَيْنَ, ذَلِكَ, تِلْكَ, أوْلَئِكَ,

(D) The subject delayed and predicate advanced

You have read in the chapter on the subject and the predicate that subject comes first and then comes the predicate as in:

The subject + the predicate.	المُبْتَدأ + الخَبْرُ
The room is big.	الغُرْفَةُ كَبِيْرَةٌ

But if you have to say: "There is a guest in the room" or "there is a thief on the top of the house" how will you say that? For such sentences the below structure is followed:

There is a guest in the house.	The subject delayed.	The predicate advanced
فِيْ الغُرْفَةِ ضَيْفٌ	ضَيْفٌ =	فِي الغُرْفَةِ +

You can see that the subject (ضَيْفٌ)has been delayed and the predicate (فِي الغُرْفَةِ)has been brought before the subject. This change of order is again an exception and happens only when the subject is an indefinite noun as evident from the above example.
Have a look at some more examples below:

There is a thief on the top of the house.	عَلي السَّقفِ لِصٌّ
There is a student in the school.	فِي المَدْرَسَةِ طَالِبٌ
There is a cat in the kitchen.	فِيْ المَطْبَخِ قِطَّة

Chapter 28
Numbers and Al-madu-du (a)

The number is called (العَدَدُ)"al-ada-du" in Arabic and a noun is followed by this number or (العَدَدُ) which is called (المَعْدُوْدُ)"al-ma-du-du".

Numbers are very important in any language and Arabic is not different in this regard. However, the number (العَدَدُ)and the noun followed by (المَعْدُوْدُ)is relatively complex in Arabic and that;s why a learner of this language finds himself or herself in a very tricky situation when it comes to deal with the issue of number. In this chapter you will learn an easy way to deal with it so that you could handle it well. This chapter is being explained step by step. You just have to follow each step very slowly and carefully.

Step 1: (One and two)

Number (العَدَدُ)and the noun followed by (المَعْدُوْدُ)–hence forth al-ma-du-du only- which comes as adjective, both will be either masculine or feminine. For these numbers the vowel mark of both the number and the noun will be the same. This is the only time when noun comes before the number. Now, observe the examples below:

	Feminine		**Masculine**
One woman Two women	إِمْرَأَةٌ وَاحِدَةٌ إِمْرَأَتَانِ إِثْنَتَانِ	One man Two men	رَجُلٌ وَاحِدٌ رَجُلَانِ إِثْنَانِ

Step 2: (Three to ten)

المَعْدُوْدُ (al-ma-du-du) of these numbers will be apposite of the number (العَدَدُ). If number is masculine then al-ma-du-du will be feminine and if the number is feminine then al-ma-du-du will be masculine. You should also remember that al-ma-du-du will be plural and shall always carry vowel mark "kas-ra" on its last letter in this case:

	Feminine		Masculine
Three women	ثَلاَثُ نِسَاءٍ	Three men	ثَلاثَةُ رِجَالٍ
Four women	أرْبَعُ نِسَاءٍ	Four men	أرْبَعَةُ رِجَالٍ
Five women	خَمْسُ نِسَاءٍ	Five men	خَمْسَةُ رِجَالٍ
Six women	سِتُّ نِسَاءٍ	Six men	سِتَّةُ رِجَالٍ
Seven women	سَبْعُ نِسَاءٍ	Seven men	سَبْعَةُ رِجَالٍ
Eight women	ثَمَانِي نِسَاءٍ	Eight men	ثَمَانِيَةُ رِجَالٍ
Nine women	تِسْعُ نِسَاءٍ	Nine men	تِسْعَةُ رِجَالٍ
Ten women	عَشرُ نِسَاءٍ	Ten men	عَشَرَةُ رِجَالٍ

Step 3: (Eleven and twelve)

Number (العَدَدُ)and al-ma-du-du (المَعْدُوْدُ)both agree with each other. So if number is masculine then al-ma-du-du will also be masculine. The same applies to feminine case as well. Al-ma-du-du in this case will be singular and shall carry vowel mark "Fat-ha with nunation":

	Feminine		Masculine
Eleven women	إحْدَي عَشرَةَ إمْرَأةً	Eleven men	احَدَ عَشرَ رَجُلاً
Twelve women	إثنَتَا عَشرَةَ إمْرَأةً	Twelve men	إثنَا عَشرَ رَجُلاً

Step 4: (Thirteen to Nineteen)

For these numbers the second part will be in agreement with al-ma-du-du (المَعْدُوْدُ)whereas the first part of it will not agree with it. So if al-ma-du-du (المَعْدُوْدُ)is masculine then the second part of the number (العَدَدُ)will also be masculine but the first part will be feminine. In case of al-ma-du-du (المَعْدُوْدُ)being feminine the opposite will be true. Al-ma-du-du (المَعْدُوْدُ)will be singular and should carry vowel mark "Fat-ha with nunation":

	Feminine		Masculine
Thirteen women	ثَلاثَ عَشَرَةَ إمْرَأةً	Thirteen men	ثَلاثَةَ عَشَرَ رَجُلاً
Fourteen women	أرْبَعَ عَشَرَةَ إمْرَأةً	Fourteen men	أرْبَعَةَ عَشَرَ رَجُلاً
Fifteen women	خَمْسَ عَشَرَةَ إمْرَأةً	Fifteen men	خَمْسَةَ عَشَرَ رَجُلاً
Sixteen women	سِتَّ عَشَرَةَ إمْرَأةً	Sixteen men	سِتَّةَ عَشَرَ رَجُلاً
Seventeen women	سَبْعَ عَشَرَةَ إمْرَأةً	Seventeen men	سَبْعَةَ عَشَرَ رَجُلاً
Eighteen women	ثَمَانِيَ عَشَرَةَ إمْرَأةً	Eighteen men	ثَمَانِيَةَ عَشَرَ رَجُلاً
Nineteen women	تِسْعَ عَشَرَةَ إمْرَأةً	Nineteen men	تِسْعَةَ عَشَرَ رَجُلاً

Step 5: (Twenty to Ninety nine)

اَلْمَعْدُوْدُ (al-ma-du-du) of all these numbers (اَلْأَعْدَادُ)will be singular and will carry “Fat-ha with nunation”. Gender of al-ma-du-du (اَلْمَعْدُوْدُ)does not change as per the number (اَلْعَدَدُ).

	Feminine		Masculine
20 women	عِشْرُوْنَ طَالِبَةً	20 men	عِشْرُوْنَ رَجُلاً
21 women	إحْدَيْ وَعِشْرُوْنَ طَالِبَةً	21 men	وَاحِدٌ وَ عِشْرُوْنَ رَجُلاً
22 women	إثْنَتَان وَعِشْرُوْنَ طَالِبَةً	22 men	إثْنَان وَ عِشْرُوْنَ رَجُلاً
23 women	ثَلاثٌ وَعِشْرُوْنَ طَالِبَةً	23 men	ثَلاثَةٌ وَ عِشْرُوْنَ رَجُلاً
24 women	أرْبَعٌ وَعِشْرُوْنَ طَالِبَةً	24 men	أرْبَعَةٌ وَعِشْرُوْنَ رَجُلاً
25 women	خَمْسٌ وَعِشْرُوْنَ طَالِبَةً	25 men	خَمْسَةٌ وَعِشْرُوْنَ رَجُلاً
26 women	سِتٌّ وَعِشْرُوْنَ طَالِبَةً	26 men	سِتَّةٌ وَعِشْرُوْنَ رَجُلاً
27 women	سَبْعٌ وَعِشْرُوْنَ طَالِبَةً	27 men	سَبْعَةٌ وَعِشْرُوْنَ رَجُلاً
28 women	ثَمَانِيٌّ وَعِشْرُوْنَ طَالِبَةً	28 men	ثَمَانِيَةٌ وَعِشْرُوْنَ رَجُلاً
29 women	تِسْعٌ وَعِشْرُوْنَ طَالِبَةً	29 men	تِسْعَةٌ وَعِشْرُوْنَ رَجُلاً
30 women	ثَلاثُوْنَ طَالِبَةً	30 men	ثَلاثُوْنَ رَجُلاً

The same pattern will continue till 99. After 30 and 40 onward you have to follow the same pattern you observed in the above examples of 20 to 30. In the below column you can see the numbers from 40 to 90. Al-ma-du-du الْمَعْدُوْدُ will always be singular and shall carry vowel mark fat-ha on its last letter:

	Feminine		Masculine
40 women	أَرْبَعُوْنَ إِمْرَأَةً	40 men	أَرْبَعُوْنَ رَجُلاً
50 women	خَمْسُوْنَ إِمْرَأَةً	50 men	خَمْسُوْنَ رَجُلاً
60 women	سِتُّوْنَ إِمْرَأَةً	60 men	سِتُّوْنَ رَجُلاً
70 women	سَبْعُوْنَ إِمْرَأَةً	70 men	سَبْعُوْنَ رَجُلاً
80 women	ثَمَانُوْنَ إِمْرَأَةً	80 men	ثَمَانُوْنَ رَجُلاً
90 women	تِسْعُوْنَ إِمْرَأَةً	90 men	تِسْعُوْنَ رَجُلاً

Step 6: (Hundred and Thousand)

الْمَعْدُوْدُ Al-ma-du-du of the above numbers (الْأَعْدَادُ)will be singular and will carry vowel mark "kas-ra with nunation". Gender of (الْمَعْدُوْدُ)is not an issue here as al-ma-du-du can be both masculine as well as feminine:

	Feminine		Masculine
100 women	مِأَةُ إِمْرَأَةٍ	100 men	مِأَةُ رَجُلٍ
1000 women	أَلْفُ إِمْرَأَةٍ	1000 men	أَلْفُ رَجُلٍ

Arabic number for Million is (مِلْيُوْن)and for Billion it is (مِلْيَار). Al-ma-du-du (الْمَعْدُوْدُ)of (مِلْيُوْنَ)will be singular with vowel mark "fat-ha" and al-ma-du-du of (مِلْيَار)will be singular with vowel mark "kas-ra".

One billion dollar	مِلْيَارُ دُوْلَار	One million men	مِلْيُوْنَ رَجُلاً

The plurals of, أَلْفٌ, مِأَةٌ and مِلْيُوْن are آلَافٌ, مِئَاتٌ and مَلَايِيْنُ respectively. The al-ma-du-du of all these numbers in plural cases also remain the same as it was in the condition of singular.

Numbers (b)

There are some more detail with regard to the numbers but you will read about those things at the higher level. However, sufficient information has been provided in this chapter which will help you understand it well.

Below in the column are given the ordinal numbers. Memorise them for daily uses:

The first	Al-awwa-lu	الأوَّلُ
The second	Ath-tha-ni-yu	الثَّانِيُ
The third	Ath-tha-lisu	الثَّالِثُ
The fourth	Ar-ra-bi-u	الرَّابِعُ
The fifth	Al-kha-mi-su	الخَامِسُ
The sixth	As-sa-di-su	السَّادِسُ
The seventh	As-sa-bi-uu	السَّابِعُ
The eighth	As-sa-mi-nu	الثَّامِنُ
The ninth	At-ta-si-uu	التَّاسِعُ
The tenth	Al-aa-shi-ru	العَاشِرُ
The eleventh	Al-hadi A-sha-ra	الحَادِي عَشَرَ
The twelth	Ath-tha-ni asha-ra	الثَّانِيْ عَشَرَ
The thirteenth	As-sa-lis asha-ra	الثَّالِثُ عَشَرَ
The fourteenth	Ar-ra-bi asha-ra	الرَّابِعُ عَشَرَ
The fifteenth	Al-kha-mis asha-ra	الخَامِسُ عَشَرَ

The countings

Twelve	إِثْنَا عَشَرَ	One	وَاحِدَةٌ
Thirteen	ثَلاثَة عَشَرَ	Two	إِثْنَتَانِ
Fourteen	أَرْبَعَة عَشَرَ	Three	ثَلاثَةٌ
Fifteen	خَمْسَة عَشَرَ	Four	أَرْبَعَةٌ

Sixteen	سِتَّة عَشَرَ	Five	خَمْسَة
Seventeen	سَبْعَة عَشَرَ	Six	سَادِسَة
Eighteen	ثَمَانِيَة عَشَرَ	Seven	سَبْعَة
Nineteen	تِسْعَة عَشَرَ	Eight	ثَمَانِيَة
Twenty	عِشْرُوْنَ	Nine	تِسْعَة
Twenty one	وَاحِدٌ وَ عِشْرُوْنَ	Ten	عَشَرَةٌ
Twenty two	إِثْنَان وَعِشْرُوْنَ	Eleven	أَحَدَ عَشَرَ

Parts of the number

One sixth	اَلسُّدُسُ	Two fold	ضِعْفَان
One seventh	اَلسُّبُعُ	Half	النِّصْفُ
One eighth	اَلثُّمُنُ	One third	الثُّلثُ
One ninth	اَلتُّسُعُ	One fourth	الرُّبُعُ
One tenth	اَلعُشْرُ	One fifth	الخُمْس

PART II
CONVERSATION

This chapter will deal with the conversation part of the book. The conversation has been designed in such a way that you can accomplish your work on your own if you happen to be in any Arabic speaking country.

But before moving to the conversation part you must know certain important ways of greeting in Arabic. These are very important for conversation as they are used on different occasions in day to today life.

Chapter 1
Greetings and courtesies

Peace be upon you (Islamic)	اَلسَّلَامُ عَلَيْكُمْ
Peace be upon you too (Islamic)	وَعَلَيْكُمُ السَّلَامُ
Good morning	صَبَاحَ الخَيْرِ\ صَبَاحَ النُّوْرِ
Good evening	مَسَاءَ الخَيْرِ \ مَسَاءَ النُّوْرِ
Hello	آلو
Welcome	أَهْلاً وَ سَهْلاً
Good night	لَيْلَةٌ سَعِيْدَةٌ
Good day	يَوْمٌ سَعِيْدٌ
Happy new year	كُلُّ عَامٍ وَ أَنْتُمْ بِخَيْرٍ
Happy Eid	عِيْدٌ سَعِيْدٌ
Wish you all the best	أَتَمَنَّي لكَ كُلَّ الخَيْرِ
Wish you luck	أَتَمَنَّيْ لكَ السَّعَادَةَ
May Allah reward you the best	جَزَاكَ اللهُ الخَيْرَ
Thanks	شُكْراً
Thank you so much	أَشْكُرُكَ شُكْراً جَزِيْلاً
Sorry	عَفْواً
I am sorry	أَرْجُو العَفْوَ
Please accept my apology	مِنْ فَضْلِكَ تَقَبَّل مِنِّي الإِعْتِذَارَ
See you soon if God willing	أَزُوْرُكَ قَرِيْباً إِنْ شَاءَ اللهُ `
See you	إِلي اللِّقَاءِ
Bye	مَعَ السَّلَامَةِ

Chapter 2
At home with family

Good morning, mom.	صَبَاحَ الخَيْرِ, يَاأُمِّي
Good morning, son.	صَبَاحَ الخَيْرِ, يَا اِبْنِيْ
Where is Khalid?	أيْنَ خَالِدٌ؟
Khalid is taking a bath in the bathroom.	خَالِدٌ يَغْتَسِلُ فِيْ الحَمَّامِ
And where is Fatima?	وَ أيْنَ فاطِمَةٌ؟
She is preparing the breakfast.	هِيَ تَطْبَخُ الفُطُوْرَ
What about my friend Faisal?	وَمَابَالُ صَدِيْقِيْ فَيْصَلَ؟
He is in the loo/toilet.	هُوَ فِي المِرْحَاضِ
But why do you ask about these?	لكِنْ لِمَاذَا تَسْأَلُ عَنْ هَؤُلاَءِ؟
We will go to the railway station together.	ذهَبُ إلِي مَحَطَةِ القِطَارِ مَعاً
When will you leave?	مَتَي تُغَادِرُوْنَ؟
We will leave at eleven o'clock sharp.	نُغَادِرُ فِي السَّاعَةِ الحَادِيَةِ عَشَرَ بِالضَّبْطِ
Will anybody travel today?	هَلْ يُسَافِرُ أحَدٌ اليَوْمَ؟
No, mom.	لا يَا أُ مِّيْ
One of our friends is visiting us today.	بَلْ يَزُوْرُنَا أحَدٌ مِنْ أصْدِقَائِنَا اليَوْمَ
Then why don't you get ready right now.	إذَنْ هَلاَّ تَسْتَعِدُّوْنَ تَوّاً

The clock has struck ten.	قَدْ ضَرَبَتِ السَّاعَةُ بِالعَاشِرَةِ
Yes, but I want to take bath first.	نَعَمْ,لكِنْ أُرِيْدُ أنْ أغْتَسِلَ أوَّلاً
Then we will have breakfast and go out.	ثُمَّ نَاكُلُ الفُطوْرَ وَ نَخْرُجُ
Good, everything is ready.	طَيِّبٌ, كُلُّ شَيْئٍ جَاهِزٌ
Eat fast and go to the station.	كُلوْا بِالسُّرْعَةِ وَاذهَبُوْا لِلمَحَطَّةِ
Will you hire the taxi?	هَلْ تَستَأجِرُوْنَ سَيَّارَةَ الْأجْرَةِ؟
Or will you take your personal car?	أمْ تَذْهَبُوْنَ بِسَيَّارَتِكُمْ الخَاصَّةِ؟
We will go in the taxi.	نَذْهَبُ فِي سَيَّارَةِ الْأجْرَةِ
We have eaten.	قَدْ أكَلنَا
Let us go or we will get late.	تَعَال نَذْهَب وَ إلاَّ نَتَأخَّرُ
We will return soon, mom.	نَعُوْدُ قرِيْبا, يَا أُمِّيْ

Chapter 3
Receiving the friend at the station

Welcome, my friend.	أهْلاً و سَهْلا, يَا صَدِيْقِي
I am very happy to see you.	سُرِرْتُ بزِيَارَتِكُمْ كَثِيْراً
We are happy too.	وَ سُرِرْنَا أيْضاً
We are waiting for you since long.	كُنَّا فِيْ إنْتِظَارِكَ مُنْذُ وَقْتٍ طوِيْلٍ
I am sorry for that.	عَفْوًا لِذَالِكَ
But the faul is not mine.	لكِنَّ الخَطأ لَيْسَ مِنْ جَانِبِيْ
The train was running very slow.	كَانَ القِطَارُ يَجْرِيْ بَطِيْئاً جِدّاً
And that's why it got delayed a lot.	وَ لِذَالِكَ تَأخَّرَ كَثِيْراً
Any ways.	عَلَيْ كُلِّ حَالٍ
How was your journey?	كَيْفَ كَانَ سَفَرُكَ؟
The journey was comfortable and good.	كَانَتِ الرِّحْلَةُ مُرِيْحَة وَ جَيِّدَةً
I thank Allah for that.	وَأشْكُرُ اللّهَ عَلي ذلِك
Let us go to home now.	تَعَال نَذْهَبْ إلي البَيْتِ الآنَ
My mom asked us to take you along.	طلَبَتْ أمِّيْ مِنَّا أنْ نَأتِيَ بكَ مَعَنَا
You will stay in my home with us.	وَأنْتَ تُقِيْمُ فِيْ بَيْتِي مَعَنَا
Sorry, friends.	مَعْذِرَةً يَا أصْدِقَائِي
I want to check in a hotel.	أرِيْدُ أنْ أنْزِلَ فِيْ فُنْدُقٍ
	لكِنْ, لايَسْمَحُ لكَ أبَوَايَ هَذَا

But my parents won't allow you this. I am under compulsion, friends.	أنَا مُضْطرٌ, يَاأصدِقائي
I will beg pardon from your kind parents.	وَ أتَقدَّمُ بالِاعْتِذار إلِيْ أبَوَيْكُمْ الكَرِيْمَيْن
It's OK.	لا بَأسَ
Then, let us go to the hotel.	إذنْ, تَعَال نَذْهَب إلي الفُنْدُق
Is the hotel close by?	هَل الفُنْدُقُ قريْبٌ؟
Yes, it is near by and cheap too.	نَعَمْ, هُوَ قريْبٌ وَرَخِيْصٌ أيْضَاً
Do you want to stay in a five star hotel?	أتُرِيْدَ أنْ تَمْكُثَ فِيْ فُنْدُقٍ ذِيْ نُجُوْمٍ خَمْسَةٍ؟
No, No, never.	لا لا, أبَداً
I am not the rich man as you know.	لسْتُ مِنَ الْأثرِيَاءِ كَمَا تَعْرِفُوْنَ

Vocabulary:

To take a bath	إغْتَسَلَ \ يَغْتَسِلُ \ اِغْتِسَالاً
The bathroom	الحَمَّامُ
The toilet\ loo	المِرْحَاضُ
What about sb	مَابَالُ فُلان
To ask	سَأَلَ \ يَسْأَلُ \ سُؤَالاً
The railway station	مَحَطَّةُ القِطَار
Together	مَعَاً
When	مَتَي
Sharp	بَالضَبْطِ

At 11 o'clock	فِيْ السَّاعَةِ الحَادِيَةِ عَشَر
To travel	سَافَرَ \ يُسَافِرُ \ مُسَافِرَةً
One of my friends	أحَدٌ مِنْ أصْدِقَائِي
A friend	صَدِيْقٌ \ أصْدِقَاءُ
To visit	زَارَ \ يَزُوْرُ \ زِيَارَةً
Then	إذَنْ
To get prepared	اِسْتَعَدَّ \ يَسْتَعِدُّ \ اِسْتِعْدَادًا
Immediately	تَوًّا
The first	أوَّلًا \ الْأوَّلُ
To come out/ go out	خَرَجَ \ يَخْرُجُ \ خُرُوْجًا
Ready	جَاهِزٌ
No	لَا
Yes	نَعَمْ
Why not	بَلَي
Speedily/ fast	بِالسُّرْعَةِ
To hire	اِسْتَأْجَرَ \ يَسْتَأْجِرُ \ اِسْتِئْجَارًا
Taxi	سَيَّارَةُ الْأُجْرَةِ
Taxi	تَاكْسِيْ
The personal car	السَّيَّارَةُ الخَاصَّةُ
To get late	تَأخَّرَ \ يَتَأخَّرُ \ تَأخُّرًا
To return	عَادَ \ يَعُوْدُ \ عَوْدَةً

The journey	الرِّحْلَةُ
Comfortable	مُرِيحة
Good	جَيِّدَةٌ
To stay	أقامَ \ يُقِيْمُ \ إقامَة
To check-in/ to descend	نَزَلَ \ يَنْزِلُ \ نُزُولاً
To allow	سَمَحَ \ يَسْمَحُ \ سَمْحاً و سَمَاحَة
The parents	الْأَبَوَان
To apologise	اِعْتَذَرَ \ يَعْتَذِرُ \ اِعْتِذَاراً
Clean	نَظِيْفٌ
Cheap	رَخِيْصٌ
Five star hotel	فُنْدُقٌ ذُوْ نُجُوْمٍ خَمْسَةٍ
Rich\ wealthy	ثَرِيٌّ \ أثْرِيَاءُ
To beg pardon	تَقَدَّمَ بالِاعْتِذار

Grammar:

The word (يَا)is used in Arabic to call out somebody. This is called حَرْفُ النِّدَاءِ (Har-fun Ni-da-e) . حَرْفُ النِّدَاءِ is followed by a noun which is called (المُنَادَي)“ Al-mu-na-da”. Look at the sturucture below:

Meaning	حَرْفُ النِّدَاءِ وَ المُنَادَي	حَرْفُ النِّدَاءِ + المُنَادَي
O boy.	يَا وَلَدُ	يَا + وَلَدُ =
O man.	يَا رَجُلُ	يَا + رَجُلُ =
O Sara.	يَا سَارَةُ	يَا + سَارَةُ =

*If the noun followed by حَرْفُ النِّدَاءِ (har-fun na-da-e) is an indefinite noun or a proper then the vowel mark of such nouns will be "Damma" as you can see in the above examples where وَلَدُ, and رَجُلُ are indefinite nouns and سَارَةُ is a proper noun.

*Besides (يَا)there are another particles or حُرُوْفُ النِّدَاءِ also. These are أَيُّهَا and أَيَّتُهَا. The particle أَيُّهَا is used with masculine noun and أَيَّتُهَا is used with feminine noun. Look at the examples below:

Meaning	حَرْفُ النِّدَيْ وَ الْمُنَادَي	حَرْفُ النِّدَيْ + الْمُنَادَيْ
O man. O student.	أَيُّهَا الرَّجُلُ أَيَّتُهَا المَرْأةُ	أَيُّهَا + الرَّجُلُ = أَيَّتُهَا + الطَّا لِبَهُ =

In this case also the vowel mark of the definite noun will be "Damma".

However, if the noun followed by حَرْفُ النِّدَاءِ is al-mudha-fu الْمُضَافُ and al-mudha-fu ilai-he الْمُضَافُ إِلَيْهِ then the vowel mark of such الْمُنَادَي الْمُضَافُ will be "Fat-ha" and الْمُضَافُ إِلَيْهِ will carry vowel mark "kas-ra" as usual. See the examples below:

Meaning	حَرْفُ النِّدَاءِ + (الْمُضَافُ + الْمُضَافُ =) الْمُنَادَي
O the student of the University. O the men of the village.	يَا + طَالِبَ + الْجَامِعَةِ = يَا طَالِبَ الْجَامِعَةِ يَا + رِجَالَ + القَرْيَةِ = يَا رِجَالَ القَرْيَةِ

Chapter 4
Booking room in a hotel

Good evening, Sir.	مَسَاءَ الخَيْر, يَا سَيِّدِي
Good evening.	مَسَاءَ الخَيْر,
Welcome.	أَهْلاً بِكَ
May I help you, Sir.	مُمْكِن أنْ أُسَاعِدَ حَضْرَتَكَ
Sure.	طَبْعًا, سَيِّدِيْ
What do you want?	مَاذَا تُرِيْدُ؟
I want to book a room in this hotel.	أُرِيْدُ حَجْزَ غُرْفَةٍ فِي هَذَاالفُنْدُق
Which type of the room do you want?	أيَّ نَوْعٍ مِنَ الغُرْفَةِ تُرِيْدُ؟
What do you mean by "type"?	مَاذَا تَقْصِدُ مِنَ النَّوْعِ؟
I mean classes of the rooms.	أقْصِدُ مِنَ النَّوْعِ دَرَجَاتِ الغُرَفِ
We have three classes of the rooms.	عِنْدَنَا غُرَفٌ مِنَ الدَّرَجَاتِ الثَّلاثَة
The first class.	-الدَّرَجَةُ الأُوْلَي
The second class.	-الدَّرَجَةُ الثَّانِيَةُ
The third class.	-الدَّرَجَةُ الثَّالِثَة
Which one of these do you want, Sir?	أيَّةَ مِنْهَا تُرِيْدُ, يَا سَيِّدِي
I want to book a second class room.	أُرِيْدُ حَجْزَ غُرْفَةٍ مِنَ الدَّرَجَةِ الثَّانِيَةِ

Do you want a single or a double bed room?	وَ هَلْ تُرِيْدُ غُرْفَة بِسَرِيْرٍ أَوْسَرِيْرَيْنِ؟
May I see the rooms first, please?	مُمْكِنْ أَنْ أَرَي الغُرَفَ أَوَّلاً, مِنْ فَضْلِكَ؟
Sure, Sir.	طَبْعَا, سَيِّدِي
I saw all the rooms.	رَأَيْتُ جَمِيْعُ الغُرَفِ
I want a single bed room.	أُرِيْدُ غُرْفَة بِسَرِيْرٍ وَاحِدٍ
What is the daily charge?	كَمْ بَدْلَ الإِيْجَارِ يَوْمِيًّا؟
Hundred dollar, Sir.	مِأَةُ دُوْلاَرٍ, حَضْرَتَك
OK.	لاَ بَأس
Please fill in the necessary details here:	مِنْ فَضْلِكَ, إِمْلَأ التَّفَاصِيْلَ اللاَّزِمَةِ هُنَا:
Where from…..	مِنْ أَيْنَ.....
Full name………	الإِسْمُ الكَامِلُ.....
Father's name……	إِسْمُ الأَبِ.....
Purpose of the visit…….	هَدَفُ الزِّيَارَةِ.....
Full address……….	العُنْوَانُ الكَامِلُ.....
Stay period……..	مُدَّةُ الإِقَامَةِ.........
Please sign over here.	مِنْ فَضْلِكَ, وَقِّعْ هُنَا
That's all, thank you.	يَكْفِي, وَشُكْراً
Here is the key of your room.	هَذَا هُوَ مِفْتَاحُ غُرْفَتِكَ
The servant will take your luggage to the room.	وَ يَحْمِلُ الخَادِمُ بَضَائِعَكَ إِلي الغُرْفَةِ

You will find everything in your room:	تَجِدُ كُلَّ شَيئٍ فِيْ غُرْفَتِك:
The towel, the soap and hot and cold water.	الفُوْطَةُ وَ الصَّابُوْنُ وَ المَاءُ السَّاخِنُ والبَارِدُ
If you want anything else.	إذا تُرِيْدُ شَيْئاً آخَرَ
Please contact the receptionist.	مِنْ فضْلِكَ إتَّصِلْ بِمُوَظَّفِ الإسْتِقْبَال
The phone is also available in your room.	الهَاتِفُ أيضاً موْجُوْدٌ فِي غُرْفَتِكَ
Thank you for your help.	شُكراً لِمُسَاعَدَتِك
Thank you.	شُكراً

Vocabulary:

Receptionist	مُوَظَّفُ الإسْتِقْبَال
To help	سَاعَدَ \ يُسَاعِدُ \ مُسَاعَدَةً
Possible	مُمْكِنٌ
To be possible	أمْكَنَ \ يُمْكِنُ \ إمْكَانَاً
Naturally	طَبْعًا \ بالطَّبْع
To book/ to reserve	حَجَزَ \ يَحْجِزُ \ حَجْزاً
Ticket booking	حَجْزُ التَّذاكِرِ
Booking of the seats	حَجْزُ المَقَاعِدِ
Room	غُرْفَةٌ \ غُرَفٌ
The first class	الدَّرَجَةُ الأوْلي
The second class	الدَّرَجَةُ الثَّانِيَةُ
The third class	الدَّرَجَةُ الثَّالِثَةُ
Single bed room	غُرْفَةٌ بسَرِيْرٍوَاحِدٍ
Double bed room	غُرْفَةٌ بسَرِيْرَيْن

Charge	بَدْلُ الإِيْجَار
Dollar	دُوْلار
To fill up	مَلَأَ \ يَمْلَأُ \ مَلْأً
Detail	تَفْصِيْلٌ \ تَفَاصِيْلُ
Necessary	اللازِمُ
The necessary detail	التَّفَاصِيْلُ اللازِمَةُ
The address	العُنْوَانُ
Full	الكَامِلُ
The period	المُدَّةُ
The stay	الإِقَامَةُ
Please	مِنْ فَضْلِكَ
To sign	وَقَّعَ \ يُوَقِّعُ \ تَوْقِيْعاً
The signature	التَّوْقِيْعُ
To be enough	كَفَيْ \ يَكْفِيْ \كِفَايَة
Key	مِفْتَاحٌ \مَفَاتِيْحُ
To find	وَجَدَ \ يَجِدُ \ وُجُوْداً
The towel	الفُوْطَةُ
The soap	الصَّابُوْنُ
The hot water	المَاءُ السَّاخِنُ
The cold water	المَاءُ البَارِدُ
To contact	اِتَّصَلَ \ يَتَّصِلُ \ اِتِّصَالاً
The contact	الإِتِّصَالُ
Communications center	مَرْكَزُ الإِتِّصَالاتِ
The phone	الهَاتِفُ
The mobile	الجَوَّالُ
The cordless	اللَّاسِلكِيْ
Available	مَوْجُوْدٌ
Not available	لَيْسَ بِمَوْجُوْدٍ

The help/ assistance	الْمُسَاعَدَةُ
The assistant professor	الْمُحَاضِرُ الْمُسَاعِدُ

Grammar:

Use of كَمْ

For expressions like "how much" or "how many" in Arabic the word (كَمْ)is used.

The noun followed by (كَمْ)receives vowel mark "fat-ha". Example:

How much amount?	كَمْ + ثَمَنَا = كَمْ ثَمَنا؟
How much price?	كَمْ + قِيْمَةَ = كَمْ قِيْمَةَ؟
How many days?	كَمْ + يَوْمَاَ = كَمْ يَوْمَاَ؟
How far?	كَمْ + بَعِيْداَ= كَمْ بَعِيْداَ؟

Use of أيٌ and أيَّةٌ

For the expression like "which one" two words (أيٌّ)and (أيَّةٌ)are used. أيٌ is used for masculine and أيَّةٌ for feminine.

أيٌ and أيَّةٌ are used as الْمُضَافُ and the noun coming after this gets vowel mark "kas-ra" because of being الْمُضَافُ إِلَيْهِ. Example:

Which color?	أيٌ لَوْنٍ؟	Which boy?	أيٌ وَلَدٍ؟
Which room?	أيَّةُ غُرْفَةٍ؟	Which doll?	أيَّةُ دُمْيَةٍ؟

أيٌ and أيَّةٌ are also used after مِنْهُ and مِنْهَا and in such cases (أيٌّ)and (أيَّةٌ)get vowel mark nunation.

Which one of them?	أيٌّ مِنْهُمْ؟
Which one of those you want?	أيَّةٌ مِنْهَا تُرِيْدُ؟

Chapter 5
Dinner in a restaurant

A new visitor to the city makes a call to his friend and asks him to come and meet him at the hotel so they can go to a restaurant for dinner together as he feels hungry.

(The phone rings)	(يَرِنُّ الْهَاتِفُ)
Hello.	آلو
This is Rashid speaking.	مَعَكَ رَاشِد,
Who Rashid?	رَاشِد مَنْ؟
Your friend who came today.	صَدِيْقُكَ الَّذِي جَاءَ الْيَوْمَ
O yes.	أيْ نعَمْ
How are you?	كَيْفُ حَالُكَ؟
I am fine, with God's grace.	أنَا طَيِّبٌ, والحَمْدُ لِلَّهِ
What made you call me up?	مَا الَّذِي حَمَلَكَ عَلي الإتِّصَال بي؟
I am hungry.	أنَاجَوْعَان
I want you to come to my hotel now.	أُرِيْدُكَ أنْ تَأْتِي إلي فُنْدُقِي الْآنَ
I want to have dinner in a restaurant tonight.	أُرِيْدُ أنْ أتَعَشَّي فِي مَطْعَمٍ هَذِهِ اللَّيْلَة
OK.	حَسَنًا
I will meet you in few seconds.	ألْقَاكَ فِيْ ثَوَانٍ

(The friend reaches)	(يَصِلُ الصَّدِيْقُ)
Thank you for coming.	شُكْراً لِمَجِيْئِكَ
Is the restaurant far away?	هَلِ المَطْعَمُ بَعِيْدٌ؟
No, it is not far away.	لا, هُوَ لَيْسَ بِبَعِيْدٍ
It is close by.	بَلْ هُوَ قَرِيْبٌ
We will walk on the feet.	نَمْشِيْ عَلَي الْأقدَامِ
And we will reach there after few minutes.	وَنَصِلُ هُنَاكَ بَعْدَ بِضْعِ دَقَائِقَ
However, we will return in a taxi.	لَكِن نَرْجِعُ فِي سَيَّارَةٍ لِلْأجْرَةِ
OK, agreed.	تَمَام, إتَّفَقنَا
(They enter into the restaurant)	(يَدْخُلَانِ فِيْ المَطْعَم)
I want to book a table for two.	أُرِيْدُ حَجْزَ طَاوِلَةٍ لِشَخْصَيْنِ
Please go ahead.	مِنْ فَضْلِكَ تَقَدَّمْ إلي الْأمَامِ
And sit on the table on the left side.	وَ اِجْلِسْ عَلي الطَّاوِلَةِ فِي الجَانِبِ الْأيْسَرِ
Thank you.	شُكْراً لَكَ
Waiter, bring a glass of water.	أيُّهَا الجَرْسُوْنُ, هَاتِ بِكُوْبٍ مِنَ المَاءِ
And where is the menu?	وَأيْنَ لَائِحَةُ الوَجْبَاتِ؟
Here it is, Sir.	تَفَضَّلْ سَيِّدِيْ
The meals include veg and non-veg foods.	وَالوَجْبَاتُ تَشْمَلُ الْأطْعِمَة النَّبَاتِيَّة وَغَيْرَ النَّبَاتِيَّة
Are you a vegetarian?	هَلْ انْتَ نَبَاتِي؟

No, I am not a vegetarian.	لا, لسْتُ بِنَبَاتِي
I will prefer the bread, the meat and the rice.	افضلُ الخُبْز و اللّحْم و الأرُزّ
And do not forget the ice-cream and the sweets in the end.	وَلا تَنسَ البُوْظة وَ الحَلاوَي فِي النّهَايَةِ
Do you want anything else, Sir?	هَلْ تُرِيدُ شيْئا آخرَ, يَا سَيِّدِي؟
No, this is enough, thanks.	لا, هذا يكفِي و شكراً
We ate and got satisfied.	أكلنَا وَ شبِعْنَا
The food was tasty.	كَانَ الطّعَامُ لذِيْذاً
The meat was tastier.	وَكَانَ اللّحْمُ ألذّ
We will go out now.	نَخْرُجُ الآن
Yes, we will pay the bill and move.	نعَمْ, نَدفعُ الفَاتُوْرَةَ وَ نَمْشِي
Here is your bill, Sir.	هَذِهِ هِيَ فَاتُوْرَتُكَ, سَيِّدِي
Where should I pay the bill?	أيْنَ أدْفعُ الفَاتُوْرَةَ؟
Go to the counter for paying the bill.	إذْهَبْ إلي النّافِذةِ لِدَفع الفَاتُوْرَة
Thank you.	شُكراً

Vocabulary:

To ring	رَنّ \ يَرِنُّ \ رَنّة
To make sb to do sth	حمَلَ \ يَحْمِلُ \ حَمْلاً عَلي
To contact	إتّصَلَ \ يَتّصِلُ \ إتّصَالاً
To be hungry	جَاعَ \ يَجُوْعُ \ جُوْعَ
Hungry	جَوْعَان
To be thirsty	عَطشَ \ يَعْطِشُ \ عَطْشاً

Thirsty	عَطْشَان
To have dinner	تَعَشَّي \ يَتَعَشَّيْ \ تَعَشِّياً
To have lunch	تَغَدَّي \ يَتَغَدَّيْ \ تَغَدِّياً
The dinner	اَلعَشَاءُ
The lunch	اَلغَدَاءُ
The restaurant	اَلمَطْعَمُ
Tonight	اللَّيْلَة
To meet	لقِيَ \ يَلقَيَ \ لِقَاءاً
Second	ثَانِيَةٌ\ ثَوَانٍ
Minute	دَقِيْقَةٌ \ دَقَائِقُ
To walk	مَشَي \ يَمْشِيْ \ مَشْياً
To reach	وَصَلَ \ يَصِلُ \ وَصْلاً ووُصُوْلاً
To return	رَجَعَ \ يَرْجِعُ \ رَجْعًا وَ رَجْعَةً وَ رُجُوْعاً
To move forward	تَقَدَّمَ \ يَتَقَدَّمُ \ تَقَدُّماً
The right side	اَلجَانِبُ الأَيْمَنُ
The left side	اَلجَانِبُ الأَيْسَرُ
Straight	عَلي طُوْلٍ
The waiter	اَلجَرْسُوْنُ
A glass of water	كُوْبٌ مِنَ المَاءِ
Menu	لاَئِحَةُ الطَّعَامِ
To include	شَمَلَ \ يَشْمَلُ \ شُمُوْلاً
Vegetarian food	اَلوَجْبَةُ النَّبَاتِيةُ
Non-vegetarian food	اَلوَجْبَةُ غَيْرُ النَّبَاتِيةِ
The bread	اَلخُبْزُ \ الأَخْبَازُ
The meat	اَللَّحْمُ \ اللُّحُوْمُ
To forget	نَسِيَ \ يَنْسَي \ نِسْيَاناً
The ice-cream	اَلبُوْظَةُ
The sweets	اَلحَلوَيْ \ الحَلاَوَي
In the end	فِي النِّهَايَةِ
To be enough	كَفَيْ \ يَكَفِيْ \ كِفَاَيَةَ وَ كَاْفِياَ
The bill	اَلفَاتُوْرَةُ
Manager of the restaurant	مُدِيْرُ المَطْعَمِ
Paying the bill	دَفعُ الفَاتُوْرَةُ

Chapter 6
In the market

Which market is cheaper in this city?	أيُّ سُوْقٍ أرْخَصُ في هَذِهِ المَدِيْنَةِ؟
Why do you ask about the market?	لِمَاذا تَسْألُ عَن السُّوْقِ؟
I want to buy few things.	اُرِيْدُ شِراءَ بَعْضِ الْأشْيَاءِ
There are many markets in this city.	هُنَاكَ أسْوَاقٌ كَثِيْرَةٌ فِي هَذِهِ الْمَدِيْنَةِ
But......market is very cheap.	لكِن سُوْقُ ......رَخِيْصَة جِدّاً
And you can find all necessary things there.	وَ يُمْكِنُ أنْ تَجِدَ جَمِيْعَ الْأشْيَاءِ اللَّازِمَةِ هُنَاكَ
This market is famous as well.	هَذِهِ السُّوْقُ مَعْرُوْفَة أيْضاً
Take a taxi to reach there.	خُذْ سَيَّارَةَ أُجْرَةٍ لِلوُصُوْلِ إلِيْهَا
The fare is not much.	وَ الْأجْرَةُ لَيْسَتْ بِكَثِيْرٍ
(Reaches a show room of clothes and shoes)	(يَصِلُ إلي مَحَلٍّ تِجَارِي لِلْأقْمِشَةِ وَ الْأحْذِيَةِ)
I want a pant and a shirt.	أُرِيْدُ قَمِيْصاً وَ بَنْطَلُوْناً
Do you want any particular color?	هَلْ تُرِيْدُ لَوْناً خَاصّاً؟
Yes.	نَعَمْ

Color of the shirt should be white. And give me a black color pant.	يَنبَغِيْ أنْ يَكُوْنَ لَوْنُ القمِيْصِ أبْيَض وَ أعْطِنِيْ البَنْطَلُوْنَ مِنْ لَوْنِ أسْوَدَ
Do you have something of the brand….	هَلْ عِنْدَكَ شَيْئٌ مِنْ صِنْفٍ......
Sorry, that brand is not available now.	عفوا, ذَالِكَ الصّنْفُ لَيس بمَوْجُوْدٍ الآن
Don't you want this one?	ألا تُرِيْدُ هَذَا؟
No, this is very expensive.	لا, هَذا غالٍ جِدّا
Do you have something cheaper than this?	هَلْ عِنْدَكَ شَيْئٌ أرْخَصُ مِنْ هَذَا؟
Yes, this is reasonable.	نَعَمْ, هَذا مُنَاسِبٌ
I want to try this pant please.	مِنْ فضْلِك, أرِيْدُ أنْ أجَرِّبَ هَذَا البَنطلُوْن
Where is the trial room?	أيْنَ غُرْفَةُ التَّجْرِبَةِ؟
It is available on the left side.	هِيَ مَوْجُوْدَةٌ فِي الجَانِبِ الأيْسَرِ
The pant is OK.	لاَ بَأسَ بِالبَنْطلُوْن
But this shirt fits tight on my body.	لكِنَّ هَذَاالقَمِيْصَ يَضِيقُ عَلي جَسَدِي
I want a shirt bigger than this?	أرِيْدُ قمِيْصاً أوْسَعَ مِنْ هَذا
This is beautiful and suits me too.	هَذا جَمِيْلٌ وَيُنَاسِبُنِي أيْضاً
How much should I pay for this shirt?	كَمْ ثَمَنا أدْفعُ لِهَذَاالقَمِيْص؟

It's cost is one thousand rupees.	قِيمَتُهُ ألفُ رُوْبِيَةٍ
And how much for the shoes?	كَمْ ثَمناً أدْفعُ لِلْأحْذِيَةِ؟
Five hundred rupees only.	خَمْسُماِءَة رُوْبِيَةٍ فقط
Do you have a hat as well?	وَهَلْ عِنْدكَ قُبَّعَة أيْضاً؟
Yes, we have many varieties of hats.	نَعَمْ, لدَيْنَا أنْوَاعٌ كَثِيْرَةٌ مِنَ القُبَّعَاتِ
I want a hat which can protect me from the sun.	أُرِيْدُ قُبَّعَة تَحْفَظنِي مِنَ الشَّمْس
This hat will suit you.	هَذِهِ القُبَّعَةُ تُنَاسِبُكَ
Then I will take it.	آخُذُهَا إذَنْ
What is the total amount?	مَا هُوَ الثَّمَنُ المَجْمُوْعُ؟
Two thousand and five hundred rupees.	ألفَانِ وَ خَمْسُماِءَة رُوْبِيَةٍ
Here it is.	هَذَا هُوَ
Thank you.	شُكْراً

Vocabulary:

Cheap	رَخِيْصٌ
Expensive	غَالٍ
To buy	شَرَيْ \ يَشْرِيْ \ شِرَاءاً
Thing	شَيئٌ \ اَشْيَاء
More	كَثِيْرٌ

Less	قَلِيْلٌ
Very	جِدّاً
All	جَمِيْعٌ
Need	حَاْجَةٌ \ حَوَائِجُ
The necessary things	اَلْحَوَائِجُ اللّاَزِمَةُ
Famous	مَعْرُوْفٌ
To know \ to recognize	عَرَفَ \ يَعْرِفُ \ عَرْفاً وَ مَعْرِفَة
To take	أَخَذَ \ يَأْخُذُ \ أَخْذاً
The fare	اَلْأُجْرَةُ
White	أَبْيَضُ \ بَيْضَاءُ
Black	أَسْوَدُ \ سَوْدَاءُ
Red	أَحْمَرُ \ حَمْرَاءُ
Blue	أَزْرَقُ \ زَرْقَاءُ
Yellow	أَصْفَرُ \ صَفْرَاءُ
Green	أَخْضَرُ \ خَضْرَاءُ
To give	أَعْطَيْ \ يُعْطِيْ \ إِعْطَاءا
Pant	بَنْطَلُوْن
Brand	صِنْفٌ \ أَصْنَافٌ
Type\ kind	نَوْعٌ \ أَنْوَاعٌ
To suit	نَاسَبَ \ يُنَاسِبُ \ مُنَاسَبَة
Suitable	مُنَاسِبٌ
To try	جَرَّبَ \ يُجَرِّبُ \ تَجْرِيْباً
Trial room	غُرْفَةُ التَّجْرِبَةِ
To be tight	ضَاقَ \ يَضِيْقُ \ ضِيْقاً
Body	جَسَدٌ \ أَجْسَادٌ
Loose	وَاسِعٌ
More loose	أَوْسَعُ
Tight	ضَيِّقٌ

Beautiful	جَمِيلٌ
Thousand	ألفٌ \ آلافٌ
The shoes	الحِذاءُ \ الأحْذِيَةُ
Five hundred rupees	خَمْسُمِاَةِ رُوْبِيةٍ
Hat	قُبَّعَة \ قُبَّعَاتٌ
To protect	حَفِظ \ يَحْفَظ \ حِفْظاً وَ حِفَاظاً
The sun	الشَّمْسُ
The moon	القمَرُ\ الأقمَارُ
The star	النَّجْمُ \ النُّجُوْمُ
The earth	الأرْضُ \ الأرَاضِي
The mountain	الجَبَلُ \ الجِبَالُ
The forest	الغَابَةُ \ الغَابَاتُ
The ocean	البَحْرُ \ الأبْحَارُ
The river	النَّهْرُ \ الأنْهَارُ
The total price	الثَّمَنُ المَجْمُوْعُ

Grammar:

Comparative degree

The pattern of comparative degree in Arabic is أفْعَلُ and a sentence will be formed as per the below structure:

The shirt is more beautiful than the pant.	القمِيْصُ + أجْمَلُ + مِنَ + البَنْطلَوْنِ

Chapter 7
In the cinema hall

We have got bored of the study today.	قَدْ سَئِمْنَا مِنَ الدِّرَاسَةِ الْيَوْمَ
Let us go to watch the movie.	تَعَال نَذْهَبْ لِمُشَاهَدَةِ السَّيْنَمَا
We will go for the night show.	نَذْهَبُ لِلعَرْض اللَّيْلي
But who will pay for the tickets?	لكِنْ مَنْ يَدْفَعُ لِلتَّذاكر؟
No one will pay on behalf of anybody.	لا يَدْفَعُ أحَدٌ لِأحَدٍ
Every one of us will watch the movie from his personal account.	كُلٌّ مِنَّا يُشَاهِدُ الفِيْلَمَ مِنْ حِسَابِهِ الذَّاتِي
Who is the hero of the movie?	مَنْ هُوَ بَطَلُ الفِيْلَمِ؟
He is a talented actor.	هُوَ مُمَثِّلٌ مُؤَهَّلٌ
And he is very famous.	وَ لَهُ شُهْرَةٌ فَائِقَة
Who is the actress?	مَنْ هِيَ البَطَلَة؟
She is an American actress.	هِيَ مُمَثِّلَة أمْرِيْكِيَّةٌ
She is acting for the first time in the Bollywood.	وتُمَثِّلُ أوَّلَ مَرَّةٍ فِي بَالِيْوُوْد

The producer of this movie gives opportunity but the attractive actresses.	مُخْرِجُ هَذَاالْفِيْلَمِ لاَ يُتِيحُ الفُرْصَةَ إلاَّ الفَاتِنَاتِ
And who is the director of the film?	وَ مَنْ هُوَ مُدِيْرُ الْفِيْلِمِ؟
I don't know, but the viewers say that the movie is very good.	لا أعْلَمُ, بَلْ يَقُوْلُ المُشَاهِدُوْنَ بِأنَّ الفِيْلَمَ جَيِّدٌ جِدًّا
We reached the cinema hall on time.	وَصَلْنَا إلِي دَارِ السَّيْنِمَا فِي المِيْعَادِ
The movie had not started yet.	مَا بَدَأَ السَّيْنَمَا حَتَّي الْآن
We bought tickets from the counter.	إشْتَرَيْنَا التَّذَاكِرَ مِنَ النَّافِذَةِ
The ticket was of the second class.	كَانَتِ التَّذَاكِرُمِنَ الدَّرَجَةِ الثَّانِيَةِ
When we entered the hall we found it dark.	لمَّا دَخَلْنَا الصَّالَة وجَدْنَاهَا مُظْلِمَةً
We searched for the seats with speculation.	بَحَثْنَا عَنِ المَقَاعِدِ بِالقِيَاس
I bumped into a person in the darkness.	وَاصْطَدَمْتُ مَعَ شَخْصٍ فِي الظُّلْمَةِ
The guard helped us sit.	سَاعَدَنَا الحَارِسُ عَلي الجُلُوْس
After few minutes the film started.	وَبَعْدَ دَقَائِقَ بَدَأَ الفِيْلَمُ

The pictures were moving on the screen.	كَانَتِ الصُوَرُ تَتَحَرَّكُ عَلَي الشَّاشَةِ
And seemed as if it were living persons.	وَ كَانَتْ تَبْدُوْ كَأَنَّهَا أَشْخَاصٌ أَحْيَاءٌ
The story of the movie was good.	قِصَّةُ الفِيْلَمِ كَانَتْ جَيِّدَةً
But I liked the dance and the songs.	لِكَنَّنِي أَحْبَبْتُ الرَّقْصَ وَ النَّغْمَاتِ
After the end of the show we felt happy.	بَعْدَ إِنْتِهَاءِ العَرْضِ شَعَرْنَا بِالفَرْحِ
And we returned to the study with new energy the next day.	وَ عُدْنَا إِلي الدِّرَاسَةِ بِقُوَّةٍ جَدِيْدَةٍ فِي اليَوْمِ التَّالِي

Vocabulary:

To get bored	سَئِمَ \ يَسْئَمُ \ سَآمَةً
Study	دِرَاسَةٌ \ دِرَاسَاتٌ
To agree	إِتَّفَقَ \ يَتَّفِقُ \ إِتِّفَاقاً
Watching the film	مُشَاهَدَةُ السِّيْنَمَا
To watch	شَاهَدَ \ يُشَاهِدُ \ مُشَاهَدَةً
The viewers	المُشَاهِدُوْنَ
The audience	المُستَمِعُوْنَ
The night show	العَرْضُ اللَّيْلِي
Ticket	تَذْكِرَةٌ \ تَذَاكِر
On his own account	عَلَي حِسَابِه
Every one of us	كُلٌّ مِنَّا
Hero	بَطَلٌ \ أَبطَالٌ

Heroine	بَطَلَةٌ \ بَطَلاَتٌ
Actor	مُمَثِّلٌ \ مُمَثِّلُونَ
Actress	مُمَثِّلَة \ مُمَثِّلاتٌ
Huge popularity	شُهْرَةٌ فَائِقَة
To act/ to perform	مَثَّلَ \ يُمَثِّلُ \تَمْثِيْلاً
First time	أوَّلُ مَرَّةٍ
Bollywood	بَالِيْوُوْد
Hollywood	هَالِيْوُوْد
Attractive woman	فَاتِنَة \ فَاتِنَاتٌ
The producer	المُخرِجُ \ المُخرِجُون
To provide	أتَاحَ \ يُتِيحُ \ إتَاحَة
Provides opportunity	يُتِيحُ الفُرْصَة
The opportunity	الفُرْصَةُ \ الفُرَصُ
Director of the film	مُدِيْرُ الفِيْلَمِ
Very good	جَيِّدٌ جِدّاً
Cinema hall	دَارُ السِّيْنَمَا
Till now/ yet	حَتَّي الآنَ
The counter	النَّافِذَةُ \ النَّوَافِذُ
The window	الشُّبَّاكُ \ الشَّبَابِيْكُ
The hall	الصَّالَهُ \ الصَّالاَتُ
Dark	مُظْلِمَة \ مُظْلِمَاتٌ
The seat	المَقْعَدُ \ المَقَاعِدُ
With speculation	بالقِيَاس
To bump into	اِصْطَدَمَ \ يَصْطَدِمُ \ اِصْطِدَاماً
To assist	سَاعَدَ \ يُسَاعِدُ \مُسَاعَدَةً
The picture	الصُّوْرَةُ \ الصُّوَرُ
To move	تَحَرَّكَ \ يَتَحَرَّكُ \ تَحَرُّكاً
The screen	الشَّاشَةُ \ الشَّاشَاتُ

The story of the film	قِصَّةُ الفِيْلِم
To like/ to love	أَحَبَّ \ يُحِبُّ \ اِحْبَاباً
To dance	رَقَصَ \ يَرْقُصُ \رَقْصاً
The dance	الرَّقْصُ
The song	النَّغْمَةُ \ النَّغْمَاتُ
To sing	غَنَّي \ يُغَنِّي \تَغْنِيَة
To end	اِنْتَهَي \ يَنْتَهِي \ اِنْتِهَاءاً
The show	العَرْضُ
The night show	العَرْضُ اللَّيْلِي
To realize/ to feel	شَعَرَ \ يَشْعُرُ\ شَعْراً وَ شُعُوْراً ب
A new energy	قُوَّةٌ جَدِيْدَةٌ
The next day	اليَوْمُ التَّالِيْ

Chapter 8
At the dispensary

It was very cold yesterday.	كَانَ البَرْدُ هُنَاكَ شَدِيْداً أَمْس
The wind was also blowing hard.	وَ كَانَتِ الرِّيْحُ تَهُبُّ بِالشِّدَّةِ أَيْضاً
Despite that I took a bath with the cold water.	مَعَ ذَلِكَ اِغْتَسَلْتُ بِالمَاءِ البَارِدِ
Now, I feel pain in my body.	الْآنَ أَشْعُرُ بِالوَجْعِ فِي جَسَدِي
And I am down with fever.	وَ أُصِبْتُ بِالحُمَّي
And my head is aching.	وَيَدْوْخُ رَأسِي
I feel pain in the chest while coughing.	وَ أَشْعُرُ بِالوَجْعِ فِي صَدْرِي عِنْدَ السُّعَال
Take me to the doctor immediately.	خُذْنِي إِلي الطَّبِيْبِ فَوْرَاً
Where is the ambulance?	أَيْنَ سَيَّارَةُ الإِسْعَافِ؟
The mother has contacted the hospital.	قَدْاِتَّصَلَتِ الأُمُّ بِالمُسْتَشْفَي
The ambulance will reach soon.	سَيَّارَةُ الإِسْعَافِ سَتَصِلُ قَرِيْباً
Father, please come.	تَفَضَّلْ يَا أَبِي
The doctor is asking for you.	يَسْأَلُ الطَّبِيْبُ عَنْكَ
He is calling you to his chamber.	وَ يَدْعُوكَ إِلي غُرْفَتِهِ

Who is the patient?	مَنْ هُوَ المَرِيْضُ؟
Doctor, I am the patient.	أنَا المرِيْضُ, أيُّها الطَّبِيْبُ
What is the problem?	مَا هِيَ المُشْكِلةُ؟
I have fever and headache.	أُصِبْتُ بالحُمَّي و الوَجْع فِي الرَّأس
And I cannot breathe well.	وَ لا أستَطِيْعُ التَّنَفُس جيِّدًا
Do you smoke?	هَلْ تُدَخِّنُ؟
Yes, I smoke but not regularly.	نَعَمْ, أدَخِّنُ لكِنْ بدُوْن إنْتَظامٍ
You must not smoke.	عَليكَ أنْ لاتُدَخِّنُ
General check-up will be done.	يَتِمُّ إجْرَاء الفَحْصِ العَامِ
The samples of your blood and urine are required.	عَيِّنَا تُ دَمِكَ وَ بَوْلِكَ مَطلُوبَة
I will give you the prescription after medical check-up.	أعْطِيْكَ الوَصْفَة الطِبِّيَّة بَعْدَ الكَشْفِ الطِّبِّي
But buy this medicine from the market.	لكِنْ إشْتَرْ هَذَاالدَّوَاءَ مِنَ السُّوْق
Take this medicine with milk.	خُذْ هَذَا الدَّوَاءَ مَعَ الحَلِيْب
This medicine is for relief only.	هَذَا الدَّوَاءُ لِلتَّسْكِيْن فقط
The blood and urine test took place.	تَمَّ إجْرَاءُ فَحْصِ الدَّمِ وَ البَوْل
You do not face any serious disease.	لاَ تُوَاجِهُ مَرَضاً خَطِيْراً

I give you this prescription.	أعْطِيْكَ هٰذِهِ الوَصْفَة الطِّبِّيَّة
If you eat all the medicines then you will get well soon.	لوْ تَأكُلُ جَمِيْعَ الأدْوِيَةِ لِتَشْفِي سَرِيْعاً
And your previous health will get back to you.	وَ تَعُوْدُ إلَيْكَ صِحَتُكَ الْأوْلي
Take bed rest for weeks.	ألزِم الفِرَاشَ لِأسْبُوْعَيْن
There is no reason for fear.	لَيْسَ هُنَاكَ سَبَبٌ لِلخَوْفِ
Thank you doctor.	شُكْراً أيُّها الطَّبِيْبُ

Vocabulary:

The dispensary	المُستَوْصَفُ
The clinic	العَيَادَةُ
The hospital	المُستَشْفَي
The coldness	البُرُوْدَةُ
The cold	البَرْدُ
Hard \ strong	شَدِيْدٌ
The wind	الرِّيْحُ \ الرِّيَاحُ
To blow	هَبَّ \ يَهُبُّ \ هُبُوْباً
The wind blows	تَهُبُّ الرِّيْحُ
To feel	شَعَرَ \ يَشْعُرُ \ شُعُوْراَب
To inflict\ to hit	أصَابَ \ يُصِيْبُ \ إصَابَةً

He is down with fever	أَصَابَتْهُ الحُمَّي
I am down with fever	أُصِبْتُ بِالحُمَّي
Dizziness	دَوْخَةٌ
Headache	أَلَمُ الرَّأس
To pain	أَوْجَعَ \ يُوْجِعُ \ إِيْجَاعاً
The cough	السُّعَالُ
Chest	صَدْرٌ \ صُدُوْرٌ
Ambulance	سَيَّارَةُ الإِسْعَافِ
The patient	المَرِيْضُ \ المَرْضَي
The problem	المُشْكِلَةُ \ المَشَاكِلُ
To breathe	تَنَفَّسَ \ يَتَنَفَّسُ \ تَنَفُّساً
Breathing	التَّنَفُّسُ
The general check-up	الفَحْصُ العَامُ
To conduct	أَجْرَي \ يُجْرِيْ \ إِجْرَاءاً
To conduct check-up	إِجْرَاءُ الفَحْص
To happen	تَمَ \ يَتِمُّ \ تَمَاماً
To smoke	دَخَّنَ \ يُدَخِّنُ \ تَدْخِيْناً
Smoking	التَّدْخِيْنُ
Regularly	بِإِنْتِظَامٍ
Irregularly	بِدُوْنِ إِنْتِظَامٍ
Sample	عَيِّنَةٌ \ عَيِّنَاتٌ

Blood samples	عَيِّنَاتُ الدَّم
Urine samples	عَيِّنَاتُ البَوْل
Prescription	الوَصْفَةُ الطِّبِّيَّةُ
Medical check-up	الكَشْفُ الطِّبِّيْ
Milk	الحَلِيْبُ
Medicine for relief	دَوَاءٌ لِلتَّسْكِيْن
Painkillers	الحُبُوْبُ المُسَكِّنَةُ
First aid	الإِسْعَافُ الأَوَّلِي
Blood test	فَحْصُ الدَّم
Urine test	فَحْصُ البَوْل
To face	وَاجَهَ \ يُوَاجِهُ \ مُوَاجَهَة
Serious disease	المَرَضُ الخَطِيْرُ
Health	الصِّحَةُ
The good health	الصِّحَةُ الجَيِّدَةُ
Reason	سَبَبٌ \ أَسْبَابٌ
The fear	الخَوْفُ
The medical certificate	الشَّهَادَةُ الطِّبِّيَّة
Specialist	إِخْتِصَاصِيٌّ

Chapter 9
At the railway station

When will you leave for the railway station, father?	مَتي تَخْرُجُ – يَاأبي- لِمَحطَةِ القِطار؟
Very little time is left for the departure of the train.	لَمْ يَبْقَ إلاَّ وَقتٌ قليْلٌ فِي مُغَادَرَةِ القِطار
I am waiting for my friend.	أنْتظِرُ لِصَدِيْقِي
He will accompany me to the station.	هُوَ يَصْطحِبُنِي إلي المَحَطَةِ
There is enough time.	هُنَاكَ وَقتٌ كَافٍ
I will reach half an hour before the departure.	سَأصِلُ نُصفَ سَاعَةٍ قبْلَ المُغَادَرَةِ
No need for hurry.	لاَ حَاجَة لِلعُجْلَةِ
Here my friend has arrived.	هَا هُوَ قدْ وَصَلَ صَدِيْقِي
Hurry up now.	عَجِّلْ الآن
Sorry, I got late.	عَفوا' تَأخَّرْتُ
Let us go.	تَعَال نَذْهَب
The taxi is parked on the door.	سَيَّارَةُ الأجْرَةِ وَاقِفَة عَلي البَابِ
What is the time now?	كَم السَّاعَةُ الآن؟
Quarter to eight.	ثمَانِيَة إلاَّ الرُبْعَ
Don't worry.	لاَ تُقلِقْ بَالكَ
We will reach soon.	سَنَصِلُ قرِيْباً

Did you take all your belongings?	هَلْ أَخَذْتَ جَمِيْعَ أَمْتِعَتِكَ؟
Yes, I did.	نَعَمْ, أَخَذْتُ
We have reached the station.	قَدْ وَصَلْنَا إلي المَحَطَّةِ
Stay in the waiting room and wait.	إبْقَ فِي غُرْفَةِ الإنْتِظار وَ انْتَظِرْ
I am going to the enquiry office.	أنَا ذَاهِبٌ إلي مَكْتَبِ الإسْتِعْلامَاتِ
Bring the suitcase and other bags closer.	قَرِّبْ المِحْفَظَة وَ الحَقائِبَ الأُخْرَي
And tie them with a strong chain.	واشْدُدْها بسِلْسِلَةٍ قَوِيَّةٍ
I will go to the ticket counter as well.	أذْهَبُ إلَيْ نَافِذَةِ التَّذَاكر أيْضاً
And will buy a ticket for you.	وَ أشْتَرِيْ تَذْكَرَةً لكَ
No need for the ticket.	لاَ حَاجَةَ لِلتَّذْكَرَةِ
My seat is already reserved.	مَقْعَدِيْ مَحْجُوْزٌ مُسَبَّقاً
Good.	طَيِّب
I asked the enquiry officer about the train.	سَألتُ مُوَظَّفَ الإسْتِعْلامَاتِ عَن القِطار
He informed me that the train is running late.	أَخْبَرَنِيْ بِأنَّ القِطارَ يَجْرِي مُتَأَخِّراً
The train will come to the platform no.1.	يَأتِي القِطارُ إلي الرَّصِيْفِ رَقم واحِد
I will take your permission now.	وَ أطْلُبُ الإذْنَ مِنْكَ الآنَ
I have some work in the market.	لِي بَعْضُ الأعْمَالِ فِي السُّوْق
I will buy some medicines.	أشْتَرِي بَعْضَ الأدْوِيَةِ

No issue, thanks.	لَا بَأس وَ شُكْراً
(He waits for few minutes then the train reaches)	(يَنتَظِرُ لِدَقائِق ثُمَّ يَصِلُ القِطارُ)
Coolie, come here.	أيُّهَا الحَمّالُ, تَعَال هُنَا
I want you to carry these luggages.	أُرِيْدُكَ أنْ تَحْمِلَ هَذِه الْأَمْتِعَة
How much amount do you want?	كَمْ مَبْلَغاً تُرِيْدُ؟
Which platform do you intend to go?	إلَي أيِّ رَصِيْفٍ تَقْصِدُ الذَّهَابَ؟
I will go to the platform no.1.	أذْهَبُ إلي الرَّصِيْفِ رَقْم وَاحِدٍ
You will pay me 150 rupees.	تَدْفَعُنِي مِأةً وَ خَمْسِيْنَ رُوْبِيَة
The charge is high.	الْأجْرَةُ مُرْتَفِعَةٌ
I will not take less than 100 rupees.	لا أقبَلُ أقَلَّ مِنْ مِأةِ رُوْبِيةٍ
Agreed.	إتَّفَقْنَا
Is your seat reserved?	هَلْ مَقْعَدُكَ مَحْجُوْزٌ؟
Yes, my seat is reserved.	نَعَمْ, مَقْعَدِيْ مَحْجُوْزٌ
In which class will you travel.	فِيْ أيِّ دَرَجَةٍ تُسَافِرُ؟
I will travel in the second class.	أُسَافِرُ فِيْ الدَّرَجَةِ الثَّانِيَةِ
(Inside the train)	(دَاخِلَ القِطار)
Can you please shift to the upper seat?	مُمْكِنْ أنْ تَنْتَقِل إلي المَقْعَدِ العَلْوِي مِن فَضْلِكَ
I want to sit on the lower seat.	أُرِيْدُ أنْ أجْلِسَ عَلي المَقْعَدِ الْأسْفَل
I feel pain in my leg.	أشْعُرُ بِالوَجْع فِي رِجْلِي

There is no problem.	لَيْسَتْ هُنَاكَ مُشْكِلَة
I will shift to the upper seat.	أَنْتَقِلُ إِلَي المَقْعَدِ العَلوي
Thank you.	شُكْراً
Where is the TTE?	وَ أَيْنَ مُفَتِّشُ التَّذَاكِر؟
I am here, Sir.	أنَا هُنَا, سَيِّدِيْ
Where is your ticket and the ID card?	أَيْنَ تَذْكَرَتُكَ وَ بِطَاقَةُ الهُوِيَّةِ؟
Here it is.	هَا هِيَ
Thank you.	شُكْراً
When will the train reach Delhi?	مَتَي يَصِلُ القِطَارُ إِلَيْ دِهْلِي؟
It will reach at 7 o'clock in the morning.	يَصِلُ فِي السَّاعَةِ السَّابِعَةِ صَبَاحاً
What is the distance between the two cities?	مَا هِيَ المَسَافَةُ بَيْنَ المَدِيْنَتَيْن؟
The distance will not be less than 520 km.	المَسَافَةُ لاتَكُوْنَ أَقَلَّ مِنْ خَمْسِمِاَةٍ وَعِشْرِيْنَ كِيْلُومِتْراً
Thank you.	شُكْراً

Vocabulary:

The rail track	السِّكَّةُ الحَدِيْدِيَّةُ
To accompany	اِصْطَحَبَ \ يَصْطَحِبُ \ اِصْطِحَاباً
Half an hour before	قَبْلَ نُصفَ سَاعَةٍ
To advise	أَشَارَ \ يُشِيْرُ \ إِشَارَةٌ عَلَي
To remain	بَقِيَ \ يَبْقَي\ بَقَاءاً
Remaining/ staying	البَقَاءُ

Waiting room	غُرْفَةُ الإِنْتِظَارِ
To head to/ to go towards	تَوَجَّهَ \ يَتَوَجَّهُ \ تَوَجُّهاً
The enquiry office	مَكْتَبُ الإِسْتِعْلَامَاتِ
To bring sth closer	قَرَّبَ \ يُقَرِّبُ \ تَقْرِيْباً
The suitcase	المِحْفَظَةُ
The bag	الحَقِيْبَةُ \ الحَقَائِبُ
The luggage	المَتَاعُ \ الْأَمْتِعَةُ
To tie	شَدَّ \ يَشُدُّ \ شَدّاً
Chain	سِلْسِلَةٌ \ سَلَاسِلُ
TV serial	السِّلْسِلَةُ التِّلْفِزْيُوْنِيَّةُ
Strong	قَوِيَّةٌ
Ticket counter	نَافِذَةُ التَّذَاكِرِ
Coolie	حَمَّالٌ \ حَمَّالُوْنَ
Carrying of the luggages	حَمْلُ الْأَمْتِعَةِ
Platform	رَصِيْفٌ \ أَرْصِفَةٌ
No. 1	رَقْمٌ وَاحِدٌ \ نِمْرَةٌ وَاحِدَةٌ
The charge	الْأُجْرَةُ
Hundred	مِائَةٌ
Fifty	خَمْسُوْنَ
High	مُرْتَفِعَةٌ
Low	مُنْخَفِضَةٌ
Less than	أَقَلُّ مِنْ
More than	أَكْثَرُ مِنْ
To agree	إِتَّفَقَ \ يَتَّفِقُ \ إِتِّفَاقاً
To reach	وَصَلَ \ يَصِلُ \ وُصُوْلاً
Late	مُتَأَخِّراً
The seat	اَلْمَقْعَدُ \ الْمَقَاعِدُ

Reserved	مَحْجُوْزٌ
To travel	سَافرَ \ يُسَافِرُ \ مُسَافرَةً
The airconditioned section	القِسْمُ المُكَيَّفُ بالهَوَاءِ
The watch\ the time	السَّاعَةُ \ السَّاعَاتُ
9 A.M	السَّاعَةُ التَّاسِعَةُ صَبَاحاً
The distance	المَسَافةُ \ المَسَافَاتُ
Five hundred and thirty	خَمْسُمِأةٍ وثَلاثُونَ
Km	كِيْلُوْ مِتْرِ
TTE	مُفَتِّشُ التَّذَاكِرِ
To get ready	اِسْتَعَدَّ \ يَسْتَعِدُّ \ اِسْتِعْدَاداً
To help	أعَانَ \ يُعِيْنُ \ إعَانَة
The help	المَعُوْنَةُ
The upper seat	المَقْعَدُ العَلَوِيْ
The middle seat	المَقْعَدُ الوَسَطِيْ
The lower seat	المَقْعَدُ السِّفْلِي
The ID card	بِطَاقَةُ الهُوِيَّةِ
To shift	اِنْتَقَلَ \ يَنْتَقِلُ \ اِنْتِقَالا
To intend	قَصَدَ \ يَقْصِدُ \ قَصْداً
Amount	مَبْلَغٌ \ مَبَالِغُ

Chapter 10
At the airport

I will go to the airport early in the morning.	أذهَبُ إلِيْ المَطَارِ فِي الصَّبَاحِ مُبَكِّراً
Is the airport close by?	هَل المَطار قريْبٌ؟
No, it is not close by.	لا, هُوَ ليْسَ بقرِيْبٍ
Rather it is far away from here.	بَل هُوَ بَعِيْدٌ مِنْ هُنَا
How long it will take to reach there?	كَمْ وَقتاً يَستَغرقُ لِلوُصُوْلِ إليْهِ؟
It will take two hours in the taxi.	هَذَا يَستَغْرقُ سَاعَتَيْنِ فِي سَيَّارَةِ الْأجْرَةِ
I must reach the airport at least one hour before the flight.	يَجِبُ أنْ أصِلَ إلِيْ المَطَارِ سَاعَةَ قبْلَ الطَّيْرَانِ عَلي الْأقلِّ
What is the time of the flight?	مَا هُوَ وَقتُ الطَّيْرَانِ؟
10:05 A.M.	السَّاعَةُ العَاشِرَةُ و خَمْسُ دَقَائِق صَبَاحاً
Where is your passport?	أيْنَ جَوَازُ سَفرِكَ؟
It is in my pocket.	هُوَ فِي جَيْبِي
And where did you put the visa?	وَأيْن وَضَعْتَ التَّأشِيْرَةَ؟
That is also available with me.	هِيَ أيْضاً مَوْجُوْدَةٌ مَعِي
Did you take all your necessary things?	هَلْ أخَذْتَ جَمِيْعَ الْأشْيَاءِ اللَّازمَةِ؟
Yes, I did.	نَعَمْ, أخَذْتُ
What is the weight of your luggages?	مَا هُوَ وَزَنُ حَقَائِبِكَ؟

I do not know.	لا أَعْلَمْ
Did you not weigh it?	أمَا قُمْتَ بوَزْنِهَا؟
No, I did not.	لاَ, مَا وَزَنْتُهَا؟
But how much weight I am allowed to carry?	لكِنْ مَا هُوَ الوَزَنُ الَّذِي يُسْمَحُ لِي بِحَمْلِهِ؟
The weight must not be more than 40 kg.	لابُدَّ أنْ لاَ يَكُوْنَ الوَزَنُ أكْثَرَ مِنْ أرْبَعِيْنَ كِيْلُوْ غِرَامِ
Did you receive your boarding pass?	هَلْ حَصَلْتَ عَلي بِطَاقَةِ الصُّعُوْدِ؟
Yes, I received it.	نَعَمْ, حَصَلْتُ عَلَيْهَا
When will the plane take-off?	مَتَي تُقْلِعُ الطَّائِرَةُ؟
It will take-off after half an hour.	تُقْلِعُ الطَّائِرَةُ بَعْدَ نُصْفِ سَاعَةٍ
When will it land?	مَتَي تَهْبِطُ؟
It will land after six hours.	تَهْبِطُ الطَّائِرَةُ بَعْدَ سِتِّ سَاعَاتٍ
And who will help me inside the plane?	وَمَنْ يُسَاعِدُنِي دَاخِلَ الطَّائِرَةِ؟
Air hostess will help you.	مُضِيْفَةُ الطَّائِرَةِ تُسَاعِدُكَ
But you must press the button for seeking help.	لكِن عَلَيْكَ أنْ تَضْغُطَ عَلِي الزِّرِّ لِطَلَبِ المُسَاعَدَةِ
Can I carry this bag with me?	هَلْ يُمْكِنُ أنْ أحْمِلَ هَذِهِ الحَقِيْبَةَ مَعِي؟
Yes, that you are allowed.	نَعَمْ, هَذَا مَسْمُوْحٌ لكَ بِهِ
Have your luggages been checked?	هَلْ تَمَّ تَفْتِيْشُ حَقَائِبِكَ؟
Yes, the checking is done.	نَعَمْ, تَمَّ التَّفْتِيْشُ

I wish you a happy journey. Bye.	أتمَنّي لكَ سَفَراً سَعِيْداً مَعَ السَّلامَةِ

Vocabulary:

Early in the morning	فِي الصَّبَاح مُبَكّراً
The airport	المَطَارُ \ المطاراتُ
To cover/ to take (time)	اِسْتَغْرَقَ \ يَسْتَغْرِقُ \ اِسْتِغْرَاقاً
Arrival	الوُصُوْلُ
Departure	المُغَادَرَةُ
To fly	طارَ \ يَطِيْرُ \ طيْرَانا
The flight	الطيْرَانُ
One hour	سَاعَةٌ
To be necessary	وَجَبَ \ يَجِبُ \ وُجُوْباً
At least	عَلي الأقلِّ
At most	عَلي الأكْثَرِ
The minimum level	اَلحَدُّ الأدْنَي
The maximum level	اَلحَدُّ الأقصَي
Flight time	مَوْعِدُالطّيْرَان
Take-off time	مَوْعِدُ الإقلاعِ
Landing time	مَوْعِدُ الهُبُوْطِ
Nine o'clock	السَّاعَةُ التَّاسِعَةُ
Five minutes	خَمْسُ دَقائِقَ
Passport	جَوَازُ السَّفَرِ
The visa	التَّأشِيْرَةُ
The necessary things	الأشْيَاءُ الضَّرُوْرِيَّةُ
The weight	الوَزَنُ \ الاوْزَانُ

To know	عَلِمَ \ يَعْلَمُ \ عِلْماً
To allow	سَمَحَ \ يَسْمَحُ \ سَمَاحَةً
Allowed	اَلْمَسْمُوْحُ بِهِ
Forty	أرْبَعُوْنَ
Kg	كِيْلُوْ غِرَام
Boarding pass	بِطَاقَةُ الصُّعُوْدِ
To receive / to get	حَصَلَ \ يَحْصُلُ \ حُصُوْلاً
To take off	أقْلَعَ \ يُقْلِعُ \ إقْلاعاً
To land	هَبَطَ \ يَهْبِطُ \ هُبُوْطاً
To assist	سَاعَدَ \ يُسَاعِدُ \ مُسَاعَدَةً
Inside the plane	دَاخِلَ الطَّائِرَةِ
Host	مُضِيْفٌ \ مُضِيْفُوْنَ
Hostess	مُضِيْفَةٌ \ مُضِيْفَاتٌ
Air hostess	مُضِيْفَةُ الطَّائِرَةِ
To check/ to search	فَتَّشَ \ يُفَتِّشُ \ تَفْتِيْشاً
Checking of the luggages	تَفْتِيْشُ الْحَقَائِبِ

Chapter 11
Opening a bank account

Did you open your account in a bank?	هَلْ فَتَحْتَ حِسَابَكَ فِي مَصْرَفٍ؟
No, I did not open my account in any bank.	لاَ, مَاْ فَتَحْتُ حِسَابِي فِي أيِّ مَصْرَفٍ
Let us go together today.	تَعَال نَذْهَبْ مَعاً اَليَوْمَ
And apply for opening of the account.	وَ نَتَقَدَّمَ بالطّلبِ لِفَتْحِ الحِسَابِ
Opening of the account is very necessary.	فَتْحُ الحِسَابِ ضَرُوْرِيٌّ جِدّاً
It helps the account holder in many ways.	يُسَاعِدَ هَذَا حَامِلَ الحِسَابِ بطرُقٍ عِدَّةٍ
The government also sends the salaries in the account directly.	تُرْسِلُ الحُكُوْمَةُ أيْضاً الرَّوَاتِبَ فِي الحِسَابِ مُبَاشَرَةً
When does the bank open?	مَتَي يَفْتَحُ المَصْرَفُ؟
Let us ask the guard of the bank.	تَعَال نَسْألُ حَارِسَ البَنْكِ
The guard says that the bank will open at 10 o'clock.	يَقُوْلُ الحَارِسُ بِأنَّ المَصْرَفَ يَفْتَحُ فِي السَّاعَةِ العَاشِرَةِ
But it is closed today.	لَكِنَّهُ مُغْلَقٌ اَليَوْمَ
Come tomorrow.	تَعَال غَداً
Who does open the account?	مَنْ يَفْتَحُ الحِسَابَ؟
Manager of the bank does that.	مُدِيْرُ المَصْرَفِ يَفْعَلُ ذَالِكَ
Fill-up this form.	إمْلَأْ هَذِهِ الِاسْتِمَارَةَ

Do you want the current account?	هَلْ تُرِيْدُ الْحِسَابَ الْجَارِي؟
No, I want the saving account.	لا, أرِيْدُ حِسَابَ الْإدِّخَار
Do you want ATM card as well?	وَ هَلْ تُرِيْدُ بطاقة الصَّرَّافِ الآلِي أيْضا؟
What is it's benefit?	مَا هِيَ فَائِدَتُهَا؟
You need not to visit the bank for withdrawal of the money.	لاتَحْتَاجُ زِيَارَةَ الْمَصرَفِ لِسَحْبِ النُّقُوْدِ
It will not be required to fill up the form for depositing money either.	وَلا تَمَسُّ الحَاجَةُ إلي مَلْإ الإسْتِمَارَةِ لِإيْدَاعِ النُّقُوْدِ
But you can do all this on your own.	بَلْ يُمْكِنُكَ أنْ تَفْعَلَ كُلَّ هَذَا بِنَفْسِكَ
Only you will visit the ATM system.	تُزُوْرُ جِهَازَ الصَّرَّافِ الآلِي فقط
And you will use this card.	وَ تَسْتَخْدِمُ هَذِهِ البطاقة
Then I want this card.	إذَنْ أرِيْدُ هَذِهِ البطاقة
Please fill up this form for that.	مِنْ فَضْلِكَ إمْلأْ إسْتِمَارَةً لَهَا
Please sign over here.	مِنْ فَضْلِكَ وَقِّعْ هُنَا
Thank you.	شُكرا
This is your account.	هَذا هُوَ حِسَابُكِ
You are our customer now.	أنْتَ زَبُوْنُنَا الآنَ
The bank will send you the ATM card via post.	يُرْسِلُ الْمَصْرَفُ بطاقة الصَّرَّافِ الآلِي عَنْ طَرِيْقِ الْبَرِيْدِ
Don,t tell any one about your password.	لاتَقُل لِأحَدٍ مَا هُوَ رَقَمُكَ السِّرِّي

Thank you for your help.	شُكْراً لِمَعُونَتِكَ
This is your personal pass book.	هَذَا هُوَ دَفْتَرُ الحِسَابِ الخَاصِّ بِكَ
And how will I withdraw money directly from the bank?	وَ كَيْفَ أَسْحَبُ النُّقُوْدَ مِنَ البَنْكِ مُبَاشَرَةً؟
You will fill up the withdrawal form.	تَمْلَأُ إِسْتِمَارَةَ السَّحْبِ
And you will write the required amount on it.	وَ تَكْتُبُ عَلَيْهَا النَّقْدَ المَطْلُوْبَ
Then you will sign on it.	ثُمَّ تُوَقِّعُ عَلَيْهَا
And you will give it to the bank officer.	وَ تَدْفَعُهَا إِلي مُوَظَّفِ المَصْرَفِ
And he will give you the required amount from your account.	وَ هُوَ يُعْطِيْكَ النَّقْدَ المَطْلُوْبَ مِنْ حِسَابِكَ
How will I deposit the money?	كَيْفَ أَقُوْمُ بِإِيْدَاعِ النُّقُوْدِ؟
You will follow the same procedures.	تَتَّبِعُ نَفْسَ الإِجْرَاءَاتِ
Only you will fill up the deposit form instead of withdrawal one.	فقطْ تَمْلَأُ إِسْتِمَارَةَ الإِيْدَاعِ بَدَلَ السَّحْبِ
Does the bank give cheque book as well?	هَلْ يُعْطِي البَنْكُ دَفْتَرَ الشِّيْكَاتِ أَيْضاً؟
Yes.	نَعَمْ
You can encash the cheques in the bank.	وَ يُمْكِنُكَ أَنْ تَصْرِفَ الشِّيْكَاتِ فِي المَصْرَفِ
Thank you for these informations.	شُكْراً لِهَذِهِ المَعْلُوْمَاتِ

Vocabulary:

The bank	المَصْرَفُ \ المَصَارِفُ
The bank	البَنْكُ \ البُنُوْكُ
To open	فَتَحَ \ يَفْتَحُ \ فَتْحاً
The account	الحِسَابُ \ الحِسَابَاتُ
The bank account	الحِسَابُ المَصْرَفِي
Guard of the bank	حَارِسُ المَصْرَفِ
Closed	مُغْلَقٌ
Open	مَفْتُوحٌ
To fill-up	مَلَأَ \ يَمْلَأُ \ مَلْأً
Form	الِإسْتِمَارَةُ \ الِإسْتِمَارَاتُ
The current account	الحِسَابُ الجَارِي
The saving account	حِسَابُ الِادِّخَارِ
The signature	الِإمْضَاءُ
Account number	رَقَمُ الحِسَابِ
To send	أَرْسَلَ \ يُرْسِلُ \ إِرْسَالاً
ATM	بطاقةُ الصَرَّافِ الآلِي
Post	البَرِيْدُ
Through	عَبْرَ
Via	عَنْ طَرِيْقِ
Password	الرَّقَمُ السِّرِّي
Password	كَلِمَةُ السِّرِّ
Pass book	دَفْتَرُ الحِسَابِ
To withdraw	سَحَبَ \ يَسْحَبُ \ سَحْباً
Withdrawal of the money	سَحْبُ النُّقُوْدِ
Directly	مُبَاشَرَةً

Indirectly	غَيْرَ مُبَاشَرَةٍ
Withdrawal form	اِسْتِمَارَةُ السَّحْبِ
The required amount	اَلنَّقْدُ المَطْلُوْبُ
To push	دَفَعَ \ يَدْفَعُ \ دَفْعاً
Employee	مُوَظَّفٌ \ مُوَظَّفُوْنَ
Bank officer	مَوَظَّفُ المَصْرَفِ
To deposit	أوْدَعَ \ يُوْدِعُ \ إِيْدِاعاً
Deposit	اَلْإِيْدَاعُ
Deposit form	اِسْتِمَارَةُ اَلْإِيْدَاع
Cheque book	دَفْتَرُ الشِّيْكَاتِ
To encash	صَرَفَ \ يَصْرِفُ \ صَرْفاً
Encashing the cheque	صَرْفُ الشِّيْكِ

PART III
EXTRA WORD POWER

This section includes topic-wise list of vocabularies divided under different headings. These are very essential for a beginner as well as a general reader who cannot consult dictionaries at the early stage of language learning.

This part of the book is also quite useful for those students who come from traditional educational academic backgrounds and struggle a lot to deal with the terminologies used in different sectors of modern life. Special attention has been paid to the needs of those who want to read Arabic newspapers and magazines or take up assignments in the newly emerged sector of medical tourism. The terminologies or words in this part cover diverse areas of medical science, finance, banking, economy, politics, science and technology and fashion.

Name of the Fruits: أَسْمَاءُ الْفَوَاكِهِ وَ الْأَثْمَار

Orange	بُرتقالٌ
Date	تمرٌ \ تُمُوْرٌ
Banana	مَوْزٌ
Apple	تُفَّاحٌ
Tamarind	تَمرٌ هِندِي
Mulberry	تُوْتٌ
Guava	جَوَافة
Walnut	جَوْزٌ
Coconut	جَوْزُ الهِنْدِ
Raisin	زَبِيْبٌ
Mango	مِشْمِشٌ
Lemon	مَانْجُوْ
Lime	لِيْمُوْن
Almond	لِيْمُوْن حَامِضٌ
Cherries	لَوْزٌ
Peanuts	كَرَزٌ
Pistachio nut	فُوْلٌ سُوْدَانِيٌ
Grapes	عِنَبٌ \ أَعْنَابٌ
Unripe	فِجٌّ
Fresh	طَازِجٌ
Watermelon	بِطِّيْخٌ
Pineapple	أَنَانَاسٌ
Fig	تِيْنٌ

Vegetables: خُضْراوات

Onion	بَصَلٌ
Sweet potato	بَطاطَا
Bringal	بَاذَنْجَان
Lady finger	بَامِيَّةٌ
Potato	بَطاطَس
Carrot	جَزْرٌ
Tomato	طَمَاطِمٌ
Lentil	عَدَسٌ
Chick-peas	حُمَّصٌ
Lettuce	خَسٌّ
Vegetables	خُضْرَوَاتٌ
Raddish	فِجْلٌ
Mushroom	فُطْرٌ
Bean	فُوْلٌ
Cucumber	خَيَارٌ
Maize	ذُرَّةٌ
Cauliflower	قُرَنْبِيْطٌ
Cabbage	كُرُنْبٌ
Olive	زَيْتُوْنٌ
Spinach	سَبَانَخٌ
Pumpkin	قَرْعٌ
Turnip	لِفْتٌ

Spices: تَوَابِلُ

Spice	تَابِلٌ \ تَوَابِلُ
Garlic	ثُوْمٌ
Pepper	فِلفِلٌ
Black pepper	فِلفِلٌ أسْوَدُ
Chilli	فِلفِلٌ حَارٌّ
Turmeric	كُرْكُمْ
Sun flower	قُرْطُمٌ
Mustard seed	خَرْدَلٌ
Saffron	زَعْفَرَانٌ
Coriander	كُزْبُرَةٌ
Salt	مِلحٌ
Mint	نَعْنَاعٌ
Sesam	سِمْسِمٌ
Ginger	زَنْجَبِيْلٌ

Animals: اَلْحَيَوَانَاتُ

Cow	بَقَرَةٌ \ أبْقَارٌ
Lion	أسَدٌ \ أُسُوْدٌ
Horse	خَيْلٌ \ خُيُوْلٌ
Horse	حِصَانٌ
Fox	ثَعْلَبٌ \ ثَعَالِبُ
Mule	بَغْلٌ
Ass/ donkey	حِمَارٌ
Zebra	حِمَارالوَحْش
Animal	حَيْوَانٌ \ حَيْوَانَاتٌ

Bull	ثَوْرٌ \ ثِيْرَانُ
Buffalo	جَامُوْسٌ \ جَوَامِيْسُ
Lamb	خَرُوْفٌ \ خِرَافٌ
Rat	جُرْدٌ \ جَرْذَانٌ
Cat	قِطَّةٌ \ قِطَطٌ
Dog	كَلْبٌ \ كِلَابٌ
Camel	جَمَلٌ \ جِمَالٌ
Pig	خِنْزِيْرٌ \ خَنَازِيْرُ
Elephant	فِيْلٌ \ أفْيَالٌ
Cheetah	نَمِرٌ \ نُمُوْرٌ
Poultry	دَاجِنَة \ دَوَاجِنُ
Wolf	ذِئْبٌ \ ذِئَابٌ
Giraffe	زَرَافَة \ زَرَافِيُ
Goat	مَعْزٌ \ غَنَمٌ \ شَاةٌ
Rat	فَأرٌ \ فِئْرَانٌ
Horse	فَرَسٌ \ أفْرَاسٌ
Hippopotamus	فَرَسُ الْبَحْرِ
Leopard	فَهْدٌ \ فُهُوْدٌ
Squirrel	سِنْجَابٌ
Monkey	قِرْدٌ \ قُرُوْدٌ
Herd of animal	قَطِيْعُ الْحَيْوَانَاتِ
Rhinoceros	كَرْكَدَن
Kangaroo	كَنْغَرٌ
Lioness	لَبْوَةٌ
Cattle	مَاشِيَةٌ \ مَوَاشِي
She-camel	نَاقَةٌ \ نُوْقٌ
Wild animal	وَحْشٌ \ وُحُوْشٌ

Birds: الطُيُوْرُ

Parrot	بَبْغَاءُ
Duck	بَطٌّ
Owl	بُوْمٌ
Pigeon/ dove	حَمَامٌ
Chicken	دَجَاجٌ
Cock	دِيْكٌ
Sparrow	عُصْفُوْرٌ \ عَصَافِيْرُ
Eagle	عُقَابٌ
Nightingale	عَنْدَلِيْبٌ \ عَنَادِلُ
Crow	غُرَابٌ \ غَرَابِيْبُ
Hawk	صَقْرٌ \ صُقُوْرٌ
Peacock	طَاوُوْسٌ
Stork	لَقلاقٌ
Ostrich	نَعَامٌ \ نَعَائِمُ
Geese	وَزٌّ
Cuckoo	وَقْوَاقٌ

Colours: اَلألوَانُ

White	أبْيَضُ
Black	أسْوَدُ
Red	أحْمَرُ
Blue	أزْرَقُ
Dark brown	أسْفَعُ
Crimson	أحْمَرُ قِرْمِزِي
Brown	أسْمَرُ

Yellow	أصْفَرُ
Orange colour	بُرْتَقَالِيُ
Bright colour	لَوْنٌ فاقِعٌ
Light colour	لَوْنٌ فاتِحٌ
Silver colour	لَوْنٌ فِضِّيٌّ
Pink colour	لَوْنٌ وَرْدِيٌّ

Human body parts: أجْزَاءُ الْجِسْمِ الْإِنْسَانِي

Head	رَأسٌ \ رُؤُوْسٌ
Hair	شَعْرٌ \ شُعُوْرٌ
Forehead	جَبِيْنٌ
Ear	أذُنٌ \ آذانٌ
Nose	أنْفٌ \ أنُوْفٌ
Eye	عَيْنٌ \ عُيُوْنٌ
Neck	عُنُقٌ \ أعْنَاقٌ
Face	وَجْهٌ \ وُجُوْهٌ
Mouth	فَمٌ
Tongue	لِسَانٌ \ ألسِنَة
Tooth	سِنٌّ \ أسْنَانٌ
Chest	صَدْرٌ \ صُدُوْرٌ
Breast	ثَدْيٌ
Bone	عَظْمٌ \ عِظَامٌ
Skin	جِلْدٌ \ جُلُوْدٌ
Stomach	بَطْنٌ \ بُطُوْنٌ
Back	ظَهْرٌ \ ظُهُوْرٌ
Waist	خَصْرٌ
Hand	يَدٌ \ أيْدِي

Leg	رِجْلٌ \ أَرْجُلٌ
Thigh	فَخِذٌ \ أَفْخَاذٌ
Finger	أَنْمُلَة \ أَنَامِلُ
Finger	إِصْبَعٌ \ أَصَابِعُ
Eyelid	جَفْنٌ \ أَجْفَانٌ
Lap	حِضْنٌ \ أَحْضَانٌ
Digestion system	جِهَازٌ هَضْمِيٌّ
Nervous system	جِهَازٌ عَصَبِيٌّ
Eyebrow	حَاجِبٌ \ حَوَاجِبُ
Cheek	خَدٌّ \ خُدُوْدٌ
Jugular vein	حَبْلُ الوَرِيْدِ
Neck	رَقَبَةٌ \ رِقَابٌ
Knee	رُكْبَةٌ \ رُكَبٌ
Arm	ذِرَاعٌ \ أَذْرُعٌ
Chin	ذِقْنٌ \ أَذْقَانٌ
Forearm	سَاعِدٌ \ سَوَاعِدُ
Foot	قَدَمٌ \ أَقْدَامٌ
Palm	رَاحَةٌ \ رَاحَاتٌ
Palm	كَفٌّ \ أَكْفَافٌ

Human relations: الْعَلَاقَاتُ الْإِنْسَانِيَّةُ

Mother	أُمٌّ \ أُمَّهَاتٌ
Father	أَبٌ \ آبَاءٌ
Grand mother	جَدَّةٌ \ جَدَّاتٌ
Grand father	جَدٌّ \ أَجْدَادٌ
Maternal grand father	جَدٌّ مِنَ الْأُمِّ
Maternal grand mother	جَدَّةٌ مِنَ الْأُمِّ

Son	إِبْنٌ \ أَبْنَاءُ
Daughter	بِنْتٌ \ بَنَاتٌ
Grand son	وَلَدُ الِإبْنِ
Grand daughter	بِنْتُ الِإبْنِ
Grand son	حَفِيْدٌ \ أَحْفَادٌ
Grand daughter	حَفِيْدَةٌ \ حَفِيْدَاتٌ
Brother	أَخٌ \ إِخْوَانٌ
Sister	أُخْتٌ \ أَخَوَاتٌ
Aunty	عَمَّةٌ \ عَمَّاتٌ
Uncle	عَمٌّ \ أَعْمَامٌ
Maternal aunt	خَالَةٌ \ خَالَاتٌ
Maternal uncle	خَالٌ \ أَخْوَالٌ
Daughter-in-law	كَنَّةٌ \ كَنَّاتٌ
Cousin brother	إِبْنُ الْعَمِّ
Cousin sister	إِبْنَةُ الْعَمِّ
Cousin brother (mother side)	إِبْنُ الخَالِ
Cousin sister (mother side)	إِبْنَةُ الخَالِ
Nephew	إِبْنُ الأَخِ
Nephew	إِبْنَةُ الأَخِ
Step mother	زَوْجَةُ الأَبِ
Step father	زَوْجُ الأُمِّ
Son-in-law	صِهْرٌ \ أَصْهَارٌ
Family	عَائِلَةٌ \ عَائِلَاتٌ
Family	أُسْرَةٌ \ أُسَرٌ

Season and directions: اَلْفُصُوْلُ وَ الْجِهَاتُ

The summer	اَلصَّيْفُ
The winter	اَلشِّتَاءُ
The spring	اَلرَّبِيْعُ
The autumn	اَلْخَرِيْفُ
The west	اَلْغَرْبُ
The east	اَلشَّرْقُ
The south	اَلْجَنُوْبُ
The north	اَلشَّمَالُ

Profession: اَلْمِهْنَةُ

Profession	مِهْنَةٌ \ مِهَنٌ
Job	وَظِيْفَةٌ \ وَظَائِفُ
Male teacher	مُعَلِّمٌ \ مُعَلِّمَاتٌ
Lady teacher	مُعَلِّمَةٌ \ مُعَلِّمَاتٌ
Male teacher	مُدَرِّسٌ \ مُدَرِّسُوْنَ
Female teacher	مُدَرِّسَةٌ \ مُدَرِّسَاتٌ
Engineer	مُهَنْدِسٌ \ مُهَنْدِسَاتٌ
Doctor	طَبِيْبٌ \ أَطِبَّاءُ
Lady doctor	طَبِيْبَةٌ \ طَبِيْبَاتٌ
Minister	وَزِيْرٌ \ وُزَرَاءُ
Police	شُرْطِيٌّ \ شُرْطِيُّوْنَ
Businessmen	رِجَالُ الْأَعْمَالِ
Coolie	حَمَّالٌ \ حَمَّالُوْنَ
Driver	سَائِقٌ \ سَائِقُوْنَ

Director	مُدِيْرٌ \ مُدَرَاءُ
Chief executive officer (CEO)	رَئِيْسٌ تَنْفِيْذِيٌّ
President	رَئِيْسٌ \ رُؤُوْسَاءُ
Prime minister	رَئِيْسُ الوُزَرَاءِ
Editor	رَئِيْسُ التَّحْرِيْرِ
Chief minister	كَبِيْرُ الوُزَرَاءِ
Barber	حَلاَّقٌ
Guard	حَارِسٌ \ حُرَّاسٌ
Producer	مُخْرِجٌ \ مُخْرِجُوْنَ
Pharmacist	صَيْدَلِيٌّ \ صَيْدَلِيُّوْنَ
Painter	رَسَّامٌ \ رَسَّامُوْنَ
Musician	مَوْسِيْقِيْ \ مَوْسِيْقِيُّوْنَ
Broadcaster	مُذِيْعٌ \ مُذِيْعُوْنَ
Pilot	طَيَّارٌ \ طَيَّارُوْنَ
Translator	مُتَرْجِمٌ \ مُتَرْجِمُوْنَ
Advocate	مُحَامِيٌ \ مُحَامِيُّوْنَ
Writer	كَاتِبٌ \ كُتَّابٌ
Money changer	صَرَّافٌ \ صَرَّافِيُّوْنَ
Correspondent	مُرَاسِلٌ \ مُرَاسِلُوْنَ
Correspondent	مُرَاسِلٌ صُحُفِيٌّ
Journalist	صَحَافِيٌّ \ صَحَافِيُّوْنَ
Professor	بُرُوْفِيْسُوْرٌ
Principal	عَمِيْدُ المَدْرَسَةِ
Mayor	عَمِيْدُ البَلَدِيَّةِ
Cook	طَبَّاخٌ \ طَبَاخُوْنَ
Supervisor	مُشْرِفٌ \ مُشْرِفُوْنَ
Judge	قَاضِي \ قُضَاةٌ

Student	طَالِبٌ \ طلاَبٌ
Accountant	مُحَاسِبٌ \ مُحَاسِبُوْنَ
Receptionist	مُوَظّفُ الْإِسْتِقْبَال

Days of the week: أيَّامُ الْأسَابِيع

Saturday	يَوْمُ السَّبْتِ
Sunday	يَوْمُ الْأحَدِ
Monday	يَوْمُ الْإِثْنَيْن
Tuesday	يَوْمُ الثّلاثَاء
Wednesday	يَوْمُ الْأرْبعَاء
Thursday	يَوْمُ الخَمِيْس
Friday	يَوْمُ الجُمُعَةِ

Name of the months: أسْمَاءُ الشُهُوْر

January	كَانُوْنُ الثّانِي/ يَنَايَرُ
February	شُبَاطٌ / فَبْرَايَرُ
March	آذَار / مَارِس
April	نِيْسَانٌ / أبْرِيْل
May	أيَّارٌ /مَايُو
June	حُزَيْرَانُ / يُوْنِيُو
July	تَمُوْز / يُوْلِيُو
August	آب / أغُسْطس
September	أيْلوْل / سِبْتِمْبَر
October	تَشْرِيْن الأوَّل / أكْتُوْبَر
November	تَشْرِيْن الثّانِي / نُوَفمْبَر
December	كَانُوْن الْأوَّل / دِسَمبَر

Things related to time and days: الْأشْيَاءُ الْمُتَعَلِّقَةُ بِالْوَقْتِ وَ الْأيَّام

Today	الْيَوْمَ
Tonight	اللَّيْلَة
Tomorrow	غَدا
Yesterday	أمْس
Day before yesterday	قَبْلَ الأمْس
Day after tomorrow	بَعْدَ الغَدِ
Last night	الْبَارِحَة
This week	هَذا الأسْبُوْعَ
The last week	الأسْبُوْعُ المَاضِي
The next year	السَّنَةُ القَادِمَةُ
Daily	يَوْمِيٌّ
Weekly	أسْبُوْعِيٌّ
Monthly	شَهْرِيٌّ
Yearly	سَنَوِيٌّ
Everyday	كُلَّ يَوْمٍ
Every week	كُلَّ أسْبُوْع
Every year	كُلَّ سَنَةٍ
Every year	كُلَّ عَامٍ
Every month	كُلَّ شَهْرٍ
Every decade	كُلَّ عَقْدٍ
Every century	كُلَّ قَرْنٍ
Second	ثَانِيَةٌ \ ثَوَانٍ
Minute	دَقِيْقَةٌ \ دَقَائِقُ
Hour	سَاعَةٌ \ سَاعَاتٌ
Day	يَوْمٌ \ أيَّامٌ

Night	لَيْلٌ \ لَيَالٍ
Morning	صَبَاحٌ
Evening	مَسَاءٌ
Noon	ظُهيْرَةٌ
After noon	بَعْدَ الظُّهيْرَةِ
Week	أُسْبُوْعٌ \ أَسَابِيْعُ
Month	شَهْرٌ \ شُهُوْرٌ
Year	سَنَةٌ \ سِنِيْنَ وَ سَنَوَاتٌ
Year	عَامٌ \ أَعْوَامٌ
Century	قَرْنٌ \ قُرُوْنٌ
Decade	عَقْدٌ \ عُقُوْدٌ
Fortnight	أُسْبُوْعَانِ
A while	بُرْهَةٌ
A moment	لَحْظَةٌ \ لَحْظَاتٌ

Words used in the media: كَلِمَاتٌ مُسْتَخْدَمَةٌ فِي الصَّحَافَةِ

No fly zone	مِنْطَقَةُ حَظْرٍ جَوِّيٍ
Credit and saving bank	بَنْكُ التَّسْلِيْفِ وَ الِادِّخَارِ
Drone	طَائِرَةٌ بِدُوْنِ طَيَّارٍ
To criticize in strong terms	اَلْإِدَانَةُ بِعِبَارَاتٍ شَدِيْدَةِ اللَّهْجَةِ
International rating agencies	وِكَالَاتُ التَّصْنِيْفِ الدُّوَلِيَّةُ
Small and medium industries	اَلْمُنْشَآتُ الصَّغِيْرَةُ وَ الْمُتَوَسِّطَةُ
Holocaust	اَلْمَحْرَقَةُ الْيَهُوْدِيَّةُ
All the options are open	جَمِيْعُ الْخِيَارَاتِ لَا تَزَالُ مَطْرُوْحَةً

Rape	إِغْتِصَابٌ
Kidnapping	اِخْتِطَافٌ
Tough competition	المُنَافسَة المُحْتَدِمَة
To have high aspirations	حَلقٌ إلي السَّمَاكِيْن
Flood prone zone	مِنْطقة أكثَرُ عُرْضَة لِلفَيْضَانَاتِ
Incubator	آلة التَّفقِيْص
Political spectrum	اَلأطيَافُ السِّيَاسِيَّة
On the eve of the election Confused	عَشِيَّة الِإنْتِخَابِ مُشرَّدُ البَال
Revolutionary guard	الحَرْسُ الثَوْري
Communal polarization	اَلِإسْتِقطَابُ الطَّائِفِي
Sovereign rating	اَلتَّصنْيْفُ السِّيَاسِي
To raise the flag of opposition	رَفعُ عَلم المُعَارَضَةِ
Futuristic approach	اَلنَّظرَةُ المُسْتَقبَلِيَّة
Public spending	اَلِإنْفاقُ الحُكُوْمِي
Developmental projects	اَلمَشَارِيْعُ التَّنمَوِيَّة
Allocation of the funds	تَخْصِيْصُ الأَمْوَال
Credibility	مِصْدَاقِيَّة
Informed sources	مَصَادِرُ مُطَّلَعَة
Highly placed sources	مَصَادِرُ رَفِيْعَة المُسْتَوَي
Medium income of the person	مُتَوَسِّطُ دَخْلِ الفَرْدِ

Wise policies	السِّيَاسَاتُ الحَكِيْمَةُ
Housing sector	قِطَاعُ الإِسْكَانِ
Education sector	قِطَاعُ التَّعْلِيْمِ
Transport sector	قِطَاعُ النَّقْلِ
High rating	التَّصْنِيْفُ المُرْتَفِعُ
Heavy investments	الإِسْتِثْمَارَاتُ الضَّخْمَةُ
Infrastructure	البِنْيَةُ التَّحْتِيَّةُ
Balanced monetary policies	سِيَاسَاتُ نَقْدِيَّةٌ مُتَوَازِنَةٌ
High regulatory capacity	القُدْرَةُ الإِشْرَافِيَّةُ العَالِيَّةُ
Financial institutions	المُؤَسَّسَاتُ المَالِيَّةُ
Well-being of the citizen	رَفَاهِيَّةُ المُوَاطِنِ
Intelligent administration	الإِدَارَةُ الحَصِيْفَةُ
High development level	دَرَجَةٌ تَنْمَوِيَّةٌ عَالِيَةٌ
Media statements	تَصْرِيْحَاتٌ صَحَافِيَّةٌ
International court of arbitration	مَحْكَمَةُ التَّحْكِيْمِ الدُّوَلِيَّةُ
Court of appeal	مَحْكَمَةُ الإِسْتِئْنَافِ
Criminal court	مَحْكَمَةُ الجِنَايَاتِ
Tribunal	مَحْكَمَةُ النَّصِّ وَ الإِبْرَامِ
Foreign direct investment (FDI)	الإِسْتِثْمَارَاتُ الأَجْنَبِيَّةُ المُبَاشِرَةُ
Modernization of the projects	تَحْدِيثُ المَشْرُوْعَاتِ
Gross domestic product	النَّاتِجُ المَحَلِّي الإِجْمَالِيُّ

Total imports	إجْمَالِي الوَارِدَاتِ
Total exports Capacity building programme	إجْمَالِي الصَّادِرَاتِ بَرْنَامَجُ التَّأهِيْل
To resort to the judiciary	اللُجُوْءُ إلي القضَاء
To resort to the arbitration	اللُجُوْءُ إلي التَّحْكيْم
Independence of the judiciary	إسْتِقلالُ القضَاء
Investment related disputes	مُنَازَعَاتُ الإسْتِثمَار
Incentives for investment projects	حَوَافِزُ لِمَشَارِيْع الاسْتِثمَار
Modern means of communication	وَسَائلُ الإتِّصَال الحَدِيْثة
Legal principals	قوَاعِدُ قانُوْنِيَّة
Flexibility	المُرُوْنَة
The Economic condition	الوَاقِعُ الإقتِصَادِيُ
The common citizen	المُوَاطِنُ العَادِيُ
Standard of living	مُستوَى المَعِيْشَةِ
Growth rate	نِسْبَةُ النُمُوِّ
Economic indices	المُؤشِرَاتُ الإقتِصَادِيَّة
Relative improvement	التَّحَسُنُ النِّسْبِيُ
The ball is now in the court of the ruling party	الكُرَةُ الآنَ فِي مَلعَبِ الحِزْبِ الحَاكِمِ
The political crisis	الأزْمَةُ السِّيَاسِيَة
Political relief	اِنْفِرَاجٌ سِيَاسِيٌ
Advanced technical features	المُوَاصَفَاتُ التَّقنِيَة المُتقدِّمَة

Audio	أَدَاةُ اِسْتِمَاع
Battery	بطارِيَّة
To recharge the battery	إعادةُ شحْن البطارِيَّةِ
Applications	تَطبيقاتٌ
Water canons	خَراطِيْمُ المِيَاهِ
Heritage zone	مِنْطقة تُرَاثِيَّة
Tear gas	الغَازُ المُسِيْلُ للدُّمُوْع
Road accident	حَادِثةُ الطَّرِيْق
Death	مَصْرَعٌ \ مَصَارِيْعُ
Injury	إصَابة \ إصَابَاتٌ
Anti tank weapon	أسْلحَة مُضَادَّةٌ لِلدَّبَّابَاتِ

Words used in the media: كَلِمَاتٌ مُسْتَخْدَمَةٌ فِي الْإِعْلَام

Communal tension	التَّوَتُّرُ الطَّائِفِيُ
Fire engine	مِضَخَّةُ الحَرِيْق
OPEC	البُلْدَانُ المُصَدِّرَةُ لِلبِتْرُوْل
Hot topic	المَوْضُوْعُ السَّاخِنُ
To ring the alarm bell	دَقُّ نَوَاقِيْس الخَطر
Moderate growth	النُّمُوُ المُعْتَدِلُ
Average speed	مُعَدِلُ السُّرْعَةِ
Shares market	سُوْقُ الْأَسْهُم

Pumping out of the petrol	ضَخُّ البِتْرُوْلِ
Water tank	مِضَخَّةُ المِيَاهِ
Geo-political situations	الْأَوْضَاعُ الجِيُوْسِيَاسِيَّةُ
Leading companies	الشَّرِكَاتُ القِيَادِيَّةُ
Long term loans	القُرُوْضُ طوِيْلَةُ الْأَمَدِ
Short term loans	القُرُوْضُ قصِيْرَةُ الْأَمَدِ
Time-bound deposits	الوَدَائِعُ الزَّمَنِيَّةُ
Saving deposits	الوَدَائِعُ الِادِّخَارِيَةُ
Bank deposits	الوَدَائِعُ المَصْرَفِيَّةُ
Inflation rate	مُعَدِلُ التَّضخُّمِ
Food prices	أَسْعَارُ الْأَغْذِيَةِ
Food inflation	تَضَخُّمُ أَسْعَارِ الْأَغْذِيَةِ
Slowing of the inflation	تَبَاطُأُ التَّضَخُّمِ
Non-petroleum exports	اَلصَّادِرَاتُ غَيْرُ النَّفْطِيَّةِ
Import of food products	وَارِدَاتُ المُنْتَجَاتِ الغِذَائِيَّةِ
Increment of supply	زِيَادَةُ العَرْضِ
Decline in the demand	تَرَاجُعُ الطَّلَبِ
Anti aircraft missile	صَارُوْخَةٌ مُضَادَّةٌ لِلطَّائِرَاتِ
Leaking	تَسْرِيْبٌ
Internation criminal court (ICC)	المَحْكَمَةُ الجِنَائِيَّةُ الدَّوَلِيَّةُ
Trial	المُحَاكَمَةُ

Fire brigade	فَرِيْقُ الإِطْفَاء
Settling of the scores	تَصْفِيَةُ الحِسَابَاتِ
Secular state	الدَّوْلَةُ العِلْمَانِيَّةُ
Exteremist elements	عَنَاصِرُ مُتَطَرِّفَة
IAEA	الوَكَالَةُ الدُّوَلِيَّةُ لِلطَّاقَةِ الذَّرِّيَةِ
Systems of governance	أَنْظِمَةُ الحُكْم
Multi-party system	نِظَامٌ مُتَعَدِّدُ الأَحْزَابِ
Pacifying the protesters	تَهْدِئَةُ المُتَظَاهِرِيْنَ
To clash with the policemen	اِصْطِدَامٌ بِرِجَالِ الشُّرْطَةِ
Eruption of the protests	اِنْدِلَاعُ المُظَاهَرَاتِ
Public park	حَدِيْقَة عَامَّة
To accept the demands	الاِسْتِجَابَةُ لِلْمُطَالَبَاتِ
Economic incomes	مَدَاخِيْلُ اِقْتِصَادِيَّة
Airlines	خُطُوْط الطَّيْرَان
Air transports	النَّاقِلَاتُ الجَوِّيَةُ
Good dishes	الأَطْبَاقُ الطَّيِّبَة
Sport clubs	الأَنْدِيَةُ الرِّيَاضِيَةُ
Football teams	الفِرَقُ الكُرَوِيَة
Military option	الخِيَارُ العَسْكَرِي
Peaceful solution	الحَلُّ السِّلْمِيُّ
Only way for solution	المَسْلَكُ الوَحِيْدُ لِلْحَلِّ

Paid forces	الْقُوَّاتُ المَأْجُوْرَةُ
Anti government protests	المُظَاهَرَاتُ المُضَادَّةُ لِلحُكُوْمَاتِ
Itinerary	بَرْنَامجُ الجَوْلَةِ
Speculations	التَّكَهُّنَاتُ
Official visit	الزِّيَارَةُ الرَّسْمِيَةُ
High level delegation	وَفْدٌ عَالِيُ المُسْتَوَي
Signing on a number of agreements	التَّوْقِيْعُ عَلَي عِدَّةِ إِتِّفَاقِيَاتٍ
Liberal trade agreement	إِتِّفَاقِيَةُ التِّجَارَةِ الحُرَّةِ
Came into effect	دَخَلَ حَيِّزَ التَّطبِيْق
Economic crisis	أَزْمَةٌ اِقْتِصَادِيَةٌ
Unemployment	البطالةُ
Top ten	العَشَرَةُ الْأَوَائِلُ
Parallel diplomacy	الدِّبْلُوْمَاسِيَّةُ المُوَازِيَةُ
Business delegation	الوَفْدُ الِاقْتِصَادِيُ
Economic issues	القَضَايَا الِاقْتِصَادِيَةُ
Combination of the delegation	تَرْكِيْبَةُ الوَفْدِ
Mining sector	قِطَاعُ التَّعْدِيْن

To behave with high confidence	تَصَرُّفٌ بِثِقَةٍ عَالِيَةٍ
Social media Sites	مَوَاقِعُ التَّوَاصُلِ الِاجْتِمَاعِيْ

Local elections	اَلِانْتِخَابَاتُ المَحَلِّيَةُ
Security forces	قُوَاتُ الأَمْنِ
Riot control police	شُرْطَةُ مُكَافِحَةُ الشَّغْبِ
Setting offices on fire	إِشْعَالُ النَّارِ فِيْ المَكَاتِبِ
Police lines	خُطُوْطُ الشُرْطَةِ
To clash with the police	إِشْتَبَكَ مَعَ الشُرْطَةِ
First known death	أَوَّلُ حَالَةِ وَفَاةٍ مَعْرُوْفَةٍ
Serious injury	إِصَابَةٌ خَطِيْرَةٌ
Talk	مُحَادَثَةٌ \ مُحَادَثَاتٌ
Dialogue	حِوَارٌ \ حِوَارَاتٌ
Freedom of expression	حُرِّيَةُ الرَّأي
Fundamental right	حَقٌّ أَسَاسِيٌّ
Internal matter	شَأْنٌ دَاخِلِيٌّ
Amnesty international	مُنَظَّمَةُ العَفْوِ الدُّوَلِيْ
Crimes against humanity	جَرَائِمُ ضِدَّالِإِنْسَانِيَةِ
Water tanks	خَزَّانَةُ المِيَاهِ
Gang war	حُرُوْبُ الطَّوَائِفِ
Political level	اَلصَّعِيْدُ السِّيَاسِي
Economic level	اَلصَّعِيْدُ الِاقْتِصَادِيُ
Political entities	الكِيَانَاتُ السِّيَاسِيَّةُ
Communal harmony	الوَلَاءَةُ الطَّائِفِيَّةُ

Dictatorial systems	أنْظِمَة تَسلُطِيَة
External dimension	البُعْدُ الخَارجِيُ
Geographic location	المَوْقِعُ الجُغْرَافِيُ
Aspiration	مَطْمَحٌ \ مَطَامِحُ
Smooth transition of the authority	اِنْتِقالٌ سَلِسٌ لِلسُلْطَةِ
Security man	رَجُلُ أمْن
Explosive situation	الوَضْعُ المُتَفَجِّرُ
Reasonal motives	دَوافِعُ مَعْقُوْلَة
Armed activity	الْعَمَلُ المُسلَحُ
Strong reservation	التَحفُّظ الشَدِيْدُ
Tense relations	العَلاَقَاتُ المُتَوَتِّرَةُ
Public works	الأشْغَالُ العُمُوْمِيَّةُ
Annual meetings	الاِجْتِماعَاتُ السَنَوِيَةُ
Boycott	مُقاطعَةٌ \ مُقاطعَاتٌ
Boycott of the forum	مُقاطعَةُ المُنْتَدَي
Inaugural session	الحَفْلُ الاِفْتِتَاحِيُ
Joint press conference	المُؤتَمرُ الصَحَافِي المُشْتَرَكُ
Bilateral relations	العَلاَقاتُ الثُنَائِيَةُ
Scheduled bilateral meetings	اللَقاءَاتُ الثُنَائِيَةُ المُبَرْمَجَةُ
Cross border crime	الجَرِيْمَةُ العَابِرَةُ لِلحُدُوْدِ
To deal with the terror threats	مُوَاجَهَةُ مَخَاطِرِ الاِرْهَابِ

Strengthening of the co-operation	تَعْزِيْزُ التَّعَاوُن
Military co-operation	اَلتَّعَاوُنُ العَسْكَرِيُ
Military leadership	اَلقِيَادَةُ العَسْكَرِيَةُ
Normalization of the relations	تَطْبِيْعُ العَلاَقَاتِ
Border problem	مُشْكِلَةُ الحُدُوْدِ
Internal problems	اَلمُشْكِلاَتُ الدَّاخِلِيَةُ
Acts of violence	أَعْمَالُ العُنْفِ
Truck	شَاحِنَةٌ \ شَاحِنَاتٌ
Provocation	اِسْتِفْزَازٌ
Ballot boxes	صَنَادِيْقُ الِاقْتِرَاعِ
Social networks	اَلشَبَكَاتُ الِاجْتِمَاعِيَةُ
To cast the vote	أدْلي بالصَّوْتِ
Rude behavior	اَلتَّعَامُلُ المُتَعَسِّفُ
Gang rape	اَلِاغْتِصَابُ الِاجْتِمَاعِيُ
Medical tests	فُحُوْصَاتٌ طِبِّيَةٌ
Suspect	اَلمُنَفِّذُ المُفْتَرَضُ
Suspects	اَلمُشْتَبَهُ فِيْهِمْ
Truck registration number	رَقَمُ تَسْجِيْلِ الشَّاحِنَةِ
Secluded place	مَكَانٌ مُنْعَزِلٌ
Heavy trucks	اَلشَّاحِنَاتُ الثَقِيْلَةُ
Local police station	مُفَوَّضِيَةُ الشُرْطَةِ المَحَلِّيَةِ

Sexual crimes	الجَرائِمُ الجِنْسِيَةُ
Sexual harassment	التَّحَرُّشُ الجِنْسِيُ
Sexual atrocities	الِاعْتِدَاءاتُ الجِنْسِيَةُ
Public opinion	الرَّأيُ العَامُ
Disclosing of the identity	كَشْفُ الهُوِيَّةِ
Simultaneous translation	التَرْجَمَةُ الفَوْرِيَةُ
Iphones	الهَوَاتِفُ الذَّكِيَةُ
Tablets	الأَجْهِزَةُ اللَّوْحِيَةُ
User ID	عُنْوَانُ المُسْتَخْدِمِ
Audio video chat	الدَّرْدَشَةُ بالصُّوْرَةِ وَ الصَّوْتِ
Group activity	العَمَلُ الجَمَاعِي
Summer vacation	الِاجَازَةُ الصَّيْفِيَّةُ
Winter vacation	الِاجَازَةُ الشَّتْوِيَةُ
Text messages	الرَّسَائِلُ النَّصِّيَةُ
E-mails	رِسَائِلُ البَرِيْدِ الِالِكْتْرُوْنِي
Attaching the pictures	دَمْجُ الصُّوَرِ
Latest offers	العُرُوْضُ النَّهائِيَةُ
Storing of the documents	تخْزِيْنُ الوَثَائِق
Business tour	رِحْلاتُ العَمَلِ
Personal expenditure	المَصَارِيْفُ الشَّخْصِيَّةُ
House arrest	الإقامَةُ الجَبْرِيَةُ

Search engine on the net.	مُحَرِّكَاتُ البَحْثِ فِي الإِنْتَرْنِيْتِ
Rights activist	النَّاشِطُ الحُقُوْقِي
Damages done to the civilian properties	أضْرَارٌ فِي المُمْتَلَكَاتِ المَدَنِيَةِ
Check post	حَاجِزُ تَفْتِيْشِ
Industrial zone	المِنْطقةُ الصِّنَاعِيَّةُ
Connecting road	الطَّرِيْقُ الوَاصِلُ
Ring road	الطَّرِيْقُ الدَّائِرِيُ
To establish the identity	التَّأكُّدُ مِنَ الهُوِيَّةِ
Armed group	مَجْمُوْعَةٌ مُسَلَّحَةٌ
Constructive dialogue	الحِوَارُ البَنَّاءُ
Genocide	إبَادَةٌ جَمَاعِيَّةٌ
Interim orders	اوَامِرُ وَقْتِيَّةٌ
Commercial papers	أوْرَاقٌ تِجَارِيَّةٌ
Making of contract	إبْرَامُ العَقْدِ
Informing the concerned authorities	إبْلاَغُ السُّلطاتِ الخَاصَّةِ
Peer group meetings	إجْتِمَاعَاتٌ بالنُّظرَاء
Order an investigation	إجْرَاءُ تَحقِيْق
Procedures	إجْرَاءَاتٌ
Selection procedures	إجْرَاءَاتُ الإخْتِيَار
Courts proceedings	إجْرَاءَاتُ المَحَاكِمِ

Provisional measures	إجْرَاءَاتٌ مُؤَقَّتَةٌ
Referral	إحَالَةٌ
To refer to the experts	إحَالَةٌ إلي الخُبَرَاءِ
Preliminary judgements	أحْكَامٌ تَمْهِيْدِيَّةٌ
Time management	إدَارَةُ الوَقْتِ
Personnel department	إدَارَةُ شُؤُوْنِ العَامِلِيْنَ
Information resource management	إدَارَةُ مَصَادِرِ المَعْلُوْمَاتِ
Public services department	إدَارَةُ الخِدْمَاتِ العَامَةِ
Technical advisors	إسْتِشَارِيُوْنَ فَنِّيُوْنَ
Consultant	إسْتِشَارِيٌ
Fee collection	تَحْصِيْلُ الرُسُوْمِ
Payment of the bill	تَسْدِيْدُ الفَاتُوْرَةِ
Preparations	تَجْهِيْزَاتٌ
Planning	تَخْطِيْطٌ \ تَخْطِيْطَاتٌ
Rehabilitation	إعَادَةُ الإسْكَانِ
Facilities and support	التَسْهِيْلاتُ وَ المَعُوْنَةُ
Amicable settlement	تَسْوِيَّةٌ وُدِّيَةٌ
Performance development	تَطْوِيْرُ الأدَاءِ
Skills development	تَطْوِيْرُ المَهَارَاتِ
Ethnic cleansing	تَطْهِيْرٌ عِرْقِيٌّ

Torture	تَعْذِيْبٌ
Compensations	تَعْوِيْضَاتٌ
Positive change	تَغَيُّرٌ إِيْجَابِيٌّ
Negotiation	تَفَاوُضٌ \ تَفَاوُضَاتٌ
Judicial investigation	التَّحْقِيْقُ القَضَائِيُ
Periodical reports	تَقَارِيْرُ دَوْرِيَّةٌ
Lobby	تَكَتُّلٌ
Financing terrorism	تَمْوِيْلُ الإِرْهَابِ
Framing of the charges	تَكْيِيفُ التُّهْمَةِ
War crimes	جَرَائِمُ حَرْبٍ
Crime	جَرِيْمَة \ جَرَائِمُ
Felony	جِنَايَةٌ \ جِنَايَاتٌ
Misdemeanor	جُنْحَةٌ
Contravention	مُخَالَفَةٌ \ مُخَالَفَاتٌ
International crimes	جَرَائِمٌ دُوَلِيَّةٌ
Court hearings	جَلَسَاتُ المَحْكَمَةِ
Caselod	حَجْمُ القَضَايَا
Backlog reduction	اَلحَدُّ مِنْ تَرَاكُمِ القَضَايَا
Judicial immunity	حَصَانَةٌ قَضَائِيَّةٌ
Diplomatic immunity	حَصَانَةٌ دِبْلُوْمَاسِيَّةٌ
Custody of the child	حَضَانَةُ الطِّفْلِ

To appear before the court	حَضَرَ أمَامَ المَحْكَمَةِ
Human rights	حُقُوْقُ الإنْسَان
Right to vote	حَقُّ التَّصْوِيْتِ
Property rights	حُقُوْقُ المِلكِيَّةِ
Breach of contract	خَرْقُ بُنُوْدِ العَقْدِ
Work plan	خُطَّةُ عَمَلٍ
Strategic plan	خُطَّة إسْتِرَاتِيْجيَّة
Academic background	خَلفِيَّة دِرَاسِيَّة
Market research	دِرَاسَةُ السُّوْق
Subsidy	دَعْمٌ
Technical support	دَعْمٌ فَنِّيٌ
Urgent case	دَعْوَي مُسْتَعْجَلَة
Legal precedents	سَوَابِقُ قَانُوْنِيَّة
Forensic science	طِبٌّ عَدْلِيٌّ
Lease contracts	عُقُوْدُ الإيْجَار
Loan contract	عَقدُ القُرُوْض
Public relations	عَلاقَاتٌ عَامَّة
Penalty	عُقُوْبَة \ عُقُوْبَاتٌ
Money laundering	غَسْلُ الأمْوَالِ \ تَبْيِيْضُ الأمْوَالِ
Coma	غَيْبُوْبَة
Termination of the contract	فَسْخُ العَقْدِ

Genocide	إبَادَةٌ جَمَاعِيَّة
Homicide	جَرِيْمَةُ قتْلٍ
Abortion	إجْهَاضٌ
Capital punishment	إعْدَامٌ
Piracy	القَرْصَنَةُ
Guarantee	كِفَالة \ كِفَالاَتٌ
Investigation committee	لجْنَةُ التَّحْقِيْق
Planning committee	لجْنَةُ التَّخْطِيْط
Fashion	المَوْضَة \ المَوْضَاتُ
Latest fashion	آخِرُ مَوْضَةٍ
Fashion designing	تَصْمِيْمُ الأزْيَاء
Fashion trends	إتِّجَاهَاتُ المَوْضَةِ
Fashion industry	صِنَاعَةُ الأزْيَاء
Model (male)	عَارِضُ الأزْيَاء
Model (female)	عَارِضَةُ الأزْيَاء
Old age home	مَأوَيْ العَجزَةِ
Mental hospital	مُسْتَشْفَي المَجَانِيْنَ
Attendant	مُمَرِّضٌ \ مُمَرِّضُوْنَ
Nurse	مُمَرِّضَةٌ \ مُمَرِّضَاتٌ
Maternity hospital	مُسْتَشْفَي الوَلاَدَةِ
Director of the hospital	مُدِيْرُ المُسْتَشْفَي

Hospital administration	إِدَارَةُ المُسْتَشْفَيَاتِ
Child care institutes	مُؤَسَّسَاتُ رِعَايَةِ الأَطْفَالِ
Children's hospital	مُسْتَشْفَي الأَطْفَال
Obstetric hospital	مُسْتَشْفَي التَّوْلِيْدِ
Private hospital	مُسْتَشْفَي خَاصٌّ
Hospital insurance	تَأمِيْنُ المُسْتَشْفَي
Hospital beds	أسِرَّةُ المُسْتَشْفَي
Soaring charges of the hospital	تَصَاعُدُ تَكَالِيْفِ العِلاَج
Epidemiologist	إِخْتِصَاصِيُّ الوَبَائِيَّاتِ
Consultant	إِسْتِشَارِيٌّ \ إِسْتِشَارِيُّوْنَ
International hospital federation	الْإِتِّحَادُ الدُّوَلِي لِلمُسْتَشْفِيَاتِ
Soar throat	اِلْتِهَابُ الحَلَق
Specific rate	الرَّسْمُ الخَاصُ
Ambulance facilities	المَرَافِقُ الْإِسْعَافِيَّةُ
Emergency	حَالَةُ الطَّوَارِئ
Blood bank	بَنْكُ الدَّم
Hospital services	خَدَمَاتُ المُسْتَشْفَي
Catchement area of a hospital	دَائِرَةُ نَشَاطِ المُسْتَشْفَي
Outpatient	العِيَادَةُ الخَارِجِيَّةُ
Hospital bed for long term stay	سَرِيْرُ المُسْتَشْفِي لِلإِقَامَةِ الطَّوِيْلَةِ
Hospital bed for short term stay	سَرِيْرُ المُسْتَشْفَي لِلإِقَامَةِ القَصِيْرَةِ

Emergency ward	قِسْمُ الطَّوَارِئ
Pharmacist	صَيْدَلَانِيٌّ
Pharmacy of the hospital	صَيْدَلَةُ المُسْتَشْفَي
Infection	العَدْوَي
Casualties department	قِسْمُ الْإِصَابَاتِ
Autopsy	تَشْرِيْحُ الجُثَّةِ
ICU (Intensive care unit)	وَحْدَةُ العِنَايَةِ المُرَكَّزَةِ
Referral hospital	مُسْتَشْفَي إحَالَةٍ
Dental hospital	مُسْتَشْفَي الْأَسْنَان
Acute care hospital	مُسْتَشْفَي الْأَمْرَاض الحَادَّةِ
Chronic disease hospital	مُسْتَشْفَي الْأَمْرَاض المُزْمِنَةِ
Mental hospital	مُسْتَشْفَي الْأَمْرَاض النَّفْسِيَّةِ
Municipality hospital	مُسْتَشْفَي البَلَدِيَّةِ
City hospital	مُسْتَشْفَي المَدِيْنَةِ
Speciality hospital	مُسْتَشْفَي تَخَصُّصِيٌّ
Government hospital	مُسْتَشْفَي حُكُوْمِيٌّ
Money	مَالٌ \ أمْوَالٌ
Currency	عُمْلَة \ عُمْلَاتٌ
Cash	نَقْدٌ \ نُقُوْدٌ
Cheque	شِيْكٌ \ شِيْكَاتٌ
To earn	كَسَبَ \ يَكْسِبُ \ كَسْبًا

To spend	صَرَفَ \ يَصْرِفُ \ صَرْفاً
To save	اِقْتَصَدَ \ يَقْتَصِدُ \ اِقْتِصَاداً
To invest	اِسْتَثْمَرَ \ يَسْتَسْمِرُ \ اِسْتِسْمَاراً
To borrow	اِسْتَلَفَ \ يَسْتَلِفُ \ اِسْتِلاَفاً
To borrow	اِسْتَعَارَ \ يَسْتَعِيْرُ \ اِسْتِعَارَةً
To lend	سَلَّفَ \ يُسَلِّفُ \ تَسْلِيْفاً
Loan	قَرْضٌ \ قُرُوْضٌ
Debt	دَيْنٌ \ دُيُوْنٌ
Credit card	بطاقةُ اِئْتِمَان
Balance	رَصِيْدٌ \ أرْصِدَةٌ
Master plan	خُطَّةٌ رَئِيْسِيَّةٌ
Mass media	وَسَائِلُ الإِعْلاَم
Mass production	الإِنْتَاجُ بِالجُمْلَةِ
Market rate of interest	سَعْرُ السُّوْق لِلْفَائِدَةِ
Labour contract	عَقْدُ العَمَل
Labour cost	تَكْلِفَةُ اليَدِ العَامِلَةِ
Labour dispute	خِلاَفٌ عُمَّالِيٌّ
Legal document	وَثِيْقَةٌ قَانُوْنِيَّةٌ
Legal status	وَضْعٌ قَانُوْنِيٌّ
Legal capital	رَأسُ المَالِ القَانُوْنِي
Leave without pay	إجَازَةٌ بِدُوْن رَاتِبٍ

Hard currency	عُمْلَةٌ صَعْبَةٌ
Health certificate	شَهَادَةٌ صِحِّيَّةٌ
Health insurance program	بَرْنَامَجٌ لِلتَّأْمِيْنِ الصِّحِّي
Headquarters	اَلْمَرْكَزُ الرَّئِيْسِيُّ
Headline	عُنْوَانُ الْعُمُوْدِ
Hawker	بَائِعٌ مُتَجَوِّلٌ
Hand-to-mouth	كَفَافِيٌّ
Handy	سَهْلُ الْمُتَنَاوَلِ
Heir apparent	وَارِثٌ شَرْعِيٌّ
Henceforth	مِنَ الْآن فَصَاعِداً
Hereafter	تَالِياً , فِيْمَا بَعْدُ
Hereby	بِهَذَا, بِمُوْجَبِ هَذِهِ (الْوَثِيْقَةِ)
Kickback	إِتَاوَةٌ \ خُوَّةٌ
Job evaluation	تَقْيِيْمُ الْوَظِيْفَةِ
Jobless	عَاطِلٌ عَنِ الْعَمَلِ
Itemized invoice	فَاتُوْرَةٌ مُفَصَّلَةُ النَّقَدَاتِ
Itinerary	بَيَانُ مَرَاحِلِ السَّفَرِ
Net weight	اَلْوَزْنُ الصَّافِي
Net price	اَلسِّعْرُ الصَّافِي
Ruling party	اَلْحِزْبُ الْحَاكِمُ
Opposition party	حِزْبُ الاخْتِلَافِ

Security council	مَجْلِسُ الأمْن
National alliance	الِائْتِلافُ الوَطَنِيُ
Ceasefire	وَقفُ إطلاَق النَّار
Prisioner	مُعْتَقلٌ \ مُعْتَقلوْن
On the sideline of the summit	عَلي هَامِش القِمَّةِ
Concerned parties	الأطرَافُ المَعْنِيَّةُ
Political solution	حَلٌّ سِيَاسِيٌّ
Military solution	حَلٌّ عَسْكَرِيٌّ
Films nominated for Oscar	الأفلامُ المُرَشَّحَةُ لِجَائِزَةِ أوْسْكَار
Best foreign movie	أفضَلُ فِلمِ أجْنَبيٌّ
Official list	قائِمَة رَسْمِيَّة
Words of thank	كَلِمَاتُ الشُكْر
The winner of the prize	الفَائِزُ بالجَائِزَةِ ·
Oscar party	حَفلةُ الأوْسْكَار
Foreign nominations	التَرْشِيْحَاتُ الأجْنَبِيَّةُ
Film making	صُنْعُ الأفلاَم
Distribution companies	شَركَاتُ التَوْزِيْع
Suicide mission	مُهِمَّة اِنْتِحَارِيَّة
Execution of the plan	تَنفِيْذُ الخُطَّةِ
He already tried	سَبَقَ أنْ حَاوَلَ
Anarchy	الفَوْضَي

The lights went off	اِنْطَفَأَتِ الْأَضْوَاءُ
Classical film	فِيْلْمٌ كَلَاسِيْكِيٌّ
The services evolved	تَطَوَّرَتِ الْخَدَمَاتُ
The services improved	تَحَسَّنَتِ الْخَدَمَاتُ
The fancy restaurants	الْمَطَاعِمُ الْفَاخِرَةُ
Sofa	أَرِيْكَةٌ \ أَرَائِكُ
Sofa for two	أَرِيْكَة تَتَّسِعُ لِشَخْصَيْن
To adjust the chairs electrically	ضَبْطُ الْمَقَاعِدِ كَهْرُبَائِيًا
Comfortable viewing angle	زَاوِيَةُ الرُّؤْيَةِ الْمُرِيْحَةِ
Drinks	مَشْرُوْبَاتٌ
Food items	مَأْكُوْلَاتٌ
Menu	قَائِمَةُ الطَّعَامِ
Film industry	صِنَاعَةُ السَّيْنَمَا
Theatres	دُوْرُ الْعَرْضِ
Entertainment	تَسْلِيَةٌ
Pleasant	مُمْتِعَةٌ
Rainy days	الْأَيَّامُ الْمُمْطِرَةُ
Suit all tastes	تُنَاسِبُ جَمِيْعَ الْأَذْوَاقِ
Screen space	مَسَاحَةُ الشَّاشَةِ
Quality of the films	نَوْعِيَّةُ الْأَفْلَامِ
Smoking ban	مَنْعُ التَّدْخِيْنِ

Switching the mobile off	إغلاَقُ الـهَاتِفِ الجَوَّال
Putting the phone on silent mode	إلغَاءُ رَنِيْن الـهَاتِفِ
Show period	فَتْرَةُ العَرْض
Parking lot	مَوْقِفُ السَّيَّارَاتِ
Partial disablement	عَجْزٌ جُزْئِيٌّ
Outstanding cheques	الشِّيْكَاتُ المُعَلَّقَةُ
Overdue	تَجَاوُزُ تَارِيْخ الِاسْتِحْقَاق
Photocopy	نُسْخَةٌ فُوْتُوْغرَافِيَّةٌ
Place of issue	مَكَانُ الِإصْدَار
Plebiscite	اِسْتِفْتَاءٌ عَامٌّ
Pick-up services	خِدْمَةُ نَقْل البَضَائِع
Tax exemption	إعْفَاءٌ ضَرِيْبِيٌّ
Tender	المُنَاقَصَةُ
Candidate	مُرَشَّحٌ
Calculator	آلَةٌ حَاسِبَةٌ
Cashier	صَرَّافٌ \ أَمِيْنُ الصُّنْدُوْق
Cash payments	مَدْفُوْعَاتٌ نَقْدِيَّةٌ
Collective effort	جُهْدٌ جَمَاعِيٌّ
Criminal negligence	إهْمَالٌ جِنَائِيٌّ
Emotional movies	أفلاَمٌ عَاطِفِيَّةٌ
Theater	المَسْرَحُ \ المَسَارِحُ